# Adhd for Kids

The Pathway to Your Kids and Adults for Success in School, College and Life

(A Self-help Workbook With Practical Suggestions for Children and Adults With Adhd)

**William Carroll**

Published by Rob Miles

© **William Carroll**

All Rights Reserved

*Adhd for Kids: The Pathway to Your Kids and Adults for Success in School, College and Life (A Self-help Workbook With Practical Suggestions for Children and Adults With Adhd)*

ISBN 978-1-990084-20-1

ISBN 978-1-990084-20-1

Legal & Disclaimer

The information contained in this book is not designed to replace or take the place of any form of medicine or professional medical advice. The information in this book has been provided for educational and entertainment purposes only.

The information contained in this book has been compiled from sources deemed reliable, and it is accurate to the best of the Author's knowledge; however, the Author cannot guarantee its accuracy and validity and cannot be held liable for any errors or omissions. Changes are periodically made to this book. You must consult your doctor or get professional medical advice before using any of the suggested remedies, techniques, or information in this book.

# Table of Contents

## Introduction

Thank you for downloading this book. The purpose of this book is to provide you with a detailed guide on what Attention Deficit Hyperactivity Disorder (ADHD), what causes ADHD, what the symptoms of ADHD are, some proven treatments of ADHD, and some techniques that will help you live a happy and productive life with ADHD. As a parent of a child diagnosed with ADHD, I understand the challenges faced by those who suffer from ADHD. This book not only addresses ADHD in children, ADHD is also prevalent in adults.

ADHD seems like it is a relatively new term, but it has been around for decades. As mental health experts have gotten better at identifying and classifying various disorders, more and more diagnosis of ADHD have become prevalent. Because of the more recent increases of these diagnosis, typically it is identified at an early age. Most persons that were born before the 1990's were considered to have personality or behavioral issues as children.

# Chapter 1: Why Is My Child Different?

We have all been told that it is unhealthy to compare your child to other children his or her age. However, this can be very hard to resist when you see droves of their peers that seem to be moving through life at a much faster rate. An eight-year-old child that can't remember to bring his books home from school or a ten-year old that can't seem to get through his or her homework without being distracted and pulled in another direction can be a scary thing for any parent to witness.

The ADHD child is often quite intelligent. They have no problem grasping the finer lessons of life and education. This is at times what perplexes a parent with a child that strays from the norm in this way. The child may have no difficulty understanding how to work their math problems, can probably write a student essay in record time, and could likely recite entire passages from a reading assignment.

The first thing one must recognize is that ADHD is not necessarily a learning disability. Many children with this condition have the ability to understand and grasp the intricacies of the world around them. However, when it comes to putting this knowledge into action, there seems to be some type of disconnect. What the child is lacking is not the ability to learn but the ability to perform effectively in their environment.

The name itself often presents some confusion for many in the child's life. Attention Deficit Hyperactivity Disorder gives the impression that the child is merely having difficulty paying attention. However, this is an oversimplified view of what's really happening. Over the last 40 years, much research has been done to prove that ADHD is not something with such an easy fix. It is more than just a child's inability to focus; it also involves the child's genetic make-up, environment, and social interactions. To claim it is just a matter of not paying attention neglects all of the other aspects of the disorder. It fails to identify the many challenges that a child may experience as he tries to fit into a fast moving world that is putting ever-increasing demands on him. This is often the reason that many with ADHD also experience bouts of frustration and anger that can be overwhelming for those around them to deal with.

Identifying the disorder is not always easy. Parents often spoke of taking their children to the doctor and having their concerns dismissed. Even medical professionals may not quickly identify the signs of ADHD. Many are often too quick to see parent's concerns as being overprotective of their child or not realistic about their expectations. Whatever the reason, it is up to the parent to insist on pushing the matter until something is done. Far too often, children are diagnosed with the disorder at a later age than could be. This delay can deprive them of years of treatment that could have put them on the right track much sooner.

Unlike physical disabilities or challenges, the child with ADHD looks perfectly normal, so people often expect him to be able to perform perfectly normal tasks. He walks, talks, and engages with his environment exactly as he should. However, as the years roll by it becomes apparent that something is not quite right. He is either out of control or is completely out of sync with the rest of the world. He has an inability to manage himself, her times, or take on additional responsibilities.

An extension of this behavior becomes evident as a state of depression. No doubt you've already seen evidence of this. A child home from school, head bowed low and their face looking totally dejected. He doesn't wish to discuss what happened during the day and may want to retreat to his room and hibernate. He knows that he is not living up to expectations and as much as he would like to, he is unable to do so it on his own, and he doesn't know why.

Your child is not lacking in intelligence and will soon see for himself that he doesn't fit in with the other children. He knows he can't keep up with the world's expectations of him. This revelation may come from your outward disappointment in him, and his behavior or from comments heard from his teacher's, relatives, siblings or anyone else that he may interact with.

The reality is however that if your child has ADHD, he is different. His brain is in a constant state of turmoil, and it is affecting him in a myriad of ways. Many people will tell you that the hyperactivity is because of eating too much sugar, it's just normal for being a kid, or he just doesn't have any boundaries. While many of these suggestions may be true, they are not the root problem for children with ADHD.

In the next chapter, we will learn how to identify the signs of ADHD and what you should know to get your doctor or other professional to understand and address your concerns. Once you begin to fully grasp the identifying marks, you'll begin to see a picture unfold that will reveal whether or not your child meets the criteria for it. If after reading this next chapter you see these markers in your child, the next step is to get a professional diagnosis to get an official diagnosis. Then you can work with him to create a plan of action that will prove to be a relief for both you and your child.

## Chapter 2: The Nutritional Approach

The nutritional approach in treating Attention Deficit Hyperactivity Disorder has been researched and debated. There are many findings that show a direct relation between the ingestion of sugar, food allergens, food additives and an increased behavioral change, in children suffering from this condition.

The role of nutrition has been mostly ignored by the public and the medical profession. Sadly, this led to disbelief from the general public, and the importance of proper nutrients remained mainly ignored. Nutritional therapy is seen just as an alternative approach, although, nutrition is the foundation of human growth.

The first to come across the idea that ADHD can be improved with a specific diet was Dr. Benjamin Feingold. He prescribed dietary changes to his patients with hives, asthma or other allergic reactions, and he noticed that the behavioral problems, that they had, were diminished. He used a diet with no artificial colorings and low in sugar. Many parents, at that time, chose to place their children under such a diet, in order to help them behave better with no drugs. Many of them were satisfied with the improvement shown by the youngsters.

Not everyone was happy with Feingold's findings, so controversy arouse. The processed-food industry (the one who had most to lose), child-behavior specialists and some pediatricians said that the success he reported with the diet wasn't supported by controlled studies. The behavioral changes could have been caused just by the placebo effect, they said, and not by the absence of chemicals and sugars.

Food additives are chemicals added to food, like antioxidants (BHT, BHA), colorings, emulsifiers, mineral salts, preservatives, flavorings and a wide range of vegetable gums.

Feingold thought that the food additives had a toxic effect, and that children affected by ADHD are different from a biochemical point of view. This has led to the assumption that the condition might be genetic. This idea is supported by the findings that one of the food colorings, called Red No. 3, used in candy and other sweets can prevent the brain from using Dopamine, this can create an increased motor activity.

With time, scientist began studying Feingold's theory. The first study was led in Pittsburgh, USA and was published in 1976. It found that four out of fifteen children suffering from ADHD improved their behavior when on a diet free of artificial colors and flavors.

Later on, studies started to look further than just additives and colorants and discovered that sugars, in all their variations, but especially aspartame and sucrose, have been linked with an increase in behavioral problems in children. Parents often report a worsening of hyperactivity after children eat candy, chocolate or drink soda. This hyperactive reaction, which comes with excessive sugar intake, can be noticed in all children, not just those suffering from ADHD.

Even if, not all patients will notice an impressive improvement on the Feingold diet, the evidence is more than enough to take under consideration the idea that food additives interact with the behavior. The diet he proposes is a healthy one, which promotes eating unrefined foods and more natural ingredients. For some patients it could be an alternative do drugs, which carry a long list of side effects and, on the long run, it's clearly healthier to at least try this diet for a couple of months. It addresses the biochemical cause of the problem, rather than just controlling the effects seen in such a condition.

Many refined sugars and especially aspartame, were linked to ADHD symptoms and with other behavioral issues in children.

The reaction children have when exposed to sucrose has been related to a series of causes, among those, a rapid increase in blood sugar that leads to hypoglycemia in a few hours, and sometimes to an allergic response.

Our view on a person that is hypoglycemic is that they are week and trembling, this might be true in people suffering from diabetes, but in children with ADHD, and healthy otherwise, will cause hyperactivity as insulin is released from the adrenal glands. This is the natural reaction of a body faced with hypoglycemia and under normal circumstances, one wouldn't become agitated but, as we've discussed before the neurotransmitters of people suffering from this condition, function a bit different. Therefore, the excessive insulin will lead to excessive restlessness. The aspartame is thought to alter the delivery of essential amino acid to the brain by elevating the serum levels, of a certain compound, called "Phenylalanine".

Many people don't understand how eating more sugar can lead to hypoglycemia so, I should explain. When a high amount of sugar is ingested, the body releases extra insulin, in order to cope with the increased glucose in the blood. The blood glucose starts dropping but the insulin remains rather high so, the level of glucose will drop even more, beneath the normal threshold.

So, we've learned that food additives and sugars can worsen the behavior of children. Now, we must understand how to improve their condition using nutrition.

## Chapter 3: Conventional Medications

Managing ADHD relies on finding the right treatment, proper medications, a sturdy support system, and undergoing behavioral therapy. Standard treatments for children with ADHD often involves medications, education, training, and counseling. It is important to talk to your doctor in order to find the most effective ADHD medications and therapy. Treatments don't actually cure ADHD, but they provide relief from the symptoms associated with the disorder.

Stimulants

Stimulant drugs are the most commonly prescribed medications for treating ADHD in children. These drugs don't increase motor activity, despite their name: they calm children down. Psychostimulants enhance brain function and balance levels of neurotransmitters. Such medications dramatically improve inattentiveness, impulsiveness, and hyperactivity—

sometimes eliminating symptoms completely.

Psychostimulants are available in capsule, skin patch, pill, and liquid form. Both short-acting and long-acting stimulant drugs are also available. Though stimulant drugs are extremely helpful in treating ADHD, they—like all drugs—come with side effects, including nausea, increased blood pressure, headache, and nervousness. However, most side effects vanish once the child's body adjusts to the stimulants.

Prescription stimulant drugs for ADHD include:

Concerta: This drug enhances the effects of dopamine and increases production of the brain chemical.

Ritalin: Also known by its generic name, methylphenidate, Ritalin treats ADHD by working on nerves and brain chemicals that contribute to hyperactivity.

Adderall: This drug facilitates the production of the brain chemicals called norepinephrine and dopamine.

Vyvanse: This drug increases one's ability to pay attention and stay focused. It also brings balance back to vital neurotransmitters.

Dexedrine: This drug helps regain focus. The drug works by making neurotransmitters last longer in the areas of the brain responsible for controlling attention and alertness.

Nonstimulants

While nonstimulant drugs are not as effective as their stimulant counterparts, they are accompanied with fewer side effects. Nonstimulant drugs help improve concentration and control impulses. Jaundice, dizziness, and fatigue are the most commonly reported side effects associated with nonstimulants.

There are three classes of nonstimulant drugs used in the treatment of ADHD:

**ADHD-Specific Nonstimulants:** These are drugs designed solely for treating ADHD, and are FDA-approved for that specific purpose. Common nonstimulants in this category include:

Strattera: This drug boosts norepinephrine—an important brain chemical—levels. This, in turn, lessens hyperactivity while increasing attention span.

Kapvay and Intuniv: These two ADHD-specific drugs have a positive influence on the brain. They improve attention, memory, and eliminate distractibility.

2.**Blood Pressure Medications:** Because some BP-targeted medications contain the same active ingredients as ADHD-specific nonstimulants, they are also effective at managing ADHD symptoms.

3.**Antidepressants:** Antidepressants combat ADHD by affecting chemicals present in the brain. This type of medication is especially beneficial for those who suffer from ADHD and mood disorders simultaneously.

Tips for Parents

Parents are responsible for ensuring the correct dosage and administration of medications to their child at the proper times. Below are several guidelines to keep in mind if your child is taking ADHD medications:

When starting medications, it is advisable to start during the weekend. This way, you'll be able to see how your child responds to the medication at home and in school.

Give the medication to your child exactly as it is prescribed to avoid the incidence of adverse reactions and other complications.

Stick to a regular schedule and have your child take his or her medication at the same time every day. Short-acting medications are usually taken 3 times per day, so make arrangements with the school clinic to ensure your child gets his required dose at the proper times. If possible, opt for long-acting medications that may be taken once a day. This way, you yourself can administer the medication at the same time every morning before school or every evening before dinner.

In the event that your child misses a dose, don't try to make up for it. Instead, have him or her take the next dose at the normal time.

Always administer medications carefully. Never let your child take medications without adult supervision.

Keep ADHD medications locked, or at the very least, out of children's reach. Overdose on stimulants can be fatal.

## Chapter 4: Signs And Symptoms Of Add And Adhd

Symptoms of ADD and ADHD may be more apparent in children. Again, this assertion could be attributed to the fact that more attention is given to children with these symptoms especially in the formative years. This should not be taken to mean that focus should be on caring for children with the condition because there are serious cases of adult ADD and ADHD that need equal attention.

Among children, ADHD is oftentimes characterized by the inability to focus, or the lack of interest, in ordinary subjects or minor details. In school, affected children have difficulty concentrating on lessons about ordinary things, but they do exhibit excited behavior when presented with something new or a twist from the ordinary. They have a tendency to be bored about certain things, and sadly that may result in poor performance when the child starts going to school. Others may exhibit hyperactivity and impulsive behavior, doing things without thinking about them first, which could lead to disastrous outcomes. Chronic forgetfulness, anxiety, low self-esteem, and anger-management issues also may be apparent among children with ADD and ADHD.

Among adults, if you have trouble concentrating, find it hard to sit still, or act in an impulsive manner without thinking things through, you may have a problem associated with ADHD. Adults also exhibit other symptoms like a feeling of inner restlessness and agitation, easily getting bored, constant fidgeting, talking excessively, and the tendency to go ahead and do several things at once but not being able to finish most of them. Adults with ADD and ADHD, like children, also show mood swings, depression, procrastination, and impulsive behavior.

Symptoms of ADD and ADHD may decrease as age progresses, but that does not necessarily mean that the disorder has been eliminated. Experts says that about 30 to 50% of people diagnosed with the disorder in childhood continue to have symptoms into adulthood. Sooner or later, the symptoms will become more noticeable later in life.

Children and adults afflicted with ADD and ADHD may also exhibit positive qualities. Among them are: a high social intelligence, a high degree of sensitivity and empathy for other people. Often, they may also show an exceptional ability to see certain things in detail and excel in certain skills more than others. Some musicians, you might have heard, have been diagnosed with ADD and ADHD but did excel in their chosen field despite the condition.

Generally, children with ADD and ADHD tend to get lower grades in school as a result of both the inattentiveness and the restlessness. Adults, meanwhile, may exhibit some form of procrastination and other negative attitudes toward work. Because of those and other factors, they have a tendency to perform less than their coworkers who do not have the disorder.

## Chapter 5: Debunking The 6 Myths Of Attention Deficit Hyperactivity Disorder

**ADHD** or attention deficit hyperactivity disorder can also be called ADD or attention deficit disorder. It is a common childhood disorder but can also affect teenager's and adults.

Adults can also have ADHD, although many people fail to recognize it. Attention deficit hyperactivity disorder in adults has the same symptoms as ADHD in children namely hyperactivity, impulsivity, and inattention. However, these symptoms are different as to how they manifest.

While children may fidget and squirm, adults with ADHD have a feeling of constant restlessness and agitation. Procrastination, disorganization, and difficulty in meeting deadlines are among the common characteristics of adults with **ADHD.**

In children, it is easier to get away with misbehaviour, as they are still young. In adults, however, ADHD symptoms can get in the way of forming social relationships as well as problems in career and finances. The cause of ADHD in adults remains a mystery.

It's unfortunate that many individuals think that people with ADHD lack willpower, are lazy, and stupid. However, the National Institute of Health, as well as the US Department of Education both, recognize ADHD as a biological disorder.

For the most part, it was only children that were originally diagnosed with Attention Deficit Hyperactivity Disorder. But adults are now being diagnosed with an adult form of the disorder on a fairly regular basis and have been since the end of the 1970's.

Additionally, when a child is diagnosed with the disorder, there is a better than average chance that they will carry ADHD with them into adulthood. Determining what is fact versus myth is usually helpful in understanding the disorder and how it functions.

The following information is some of the more common myths and facts regarding Attention Deficit Hyperactivity Disorder that you should be aware of:

**Myth #1: Children Eventually Outgrow ADHD - FALSE**. Roughly 70% of children who are diagnosed with ADHD will continue to have the symptoms into there adolescent years while 60% of them will still have the disorder as adults.

**Myth #2: ADHD Indicates A Lack Of Willpower And Is Not Really A Disorder - FALSE.** Attention Deficit Hyperactivity Disorder is a neurological disorder. Despite some of the controversy and speculation regarding ADHD, that much has been proven as the brain's management systems are experiencing a chemical imbalance when the disorder is present.

**Myth #3: Only Males Are Affected And Diagnosed with ADHD - FALSE.** Female's are just as likely to succumb to the disorder. This misconception stems from the fact that teachers who refer students to an ADHD type of education program have a pre-conceived notion about boys and behavioural issues during their developmental years.

**Myth #4: ADHD Results From Bad Parenting - FALSE.** Attention Deficit Hyperactivity Disorder is not caused by the type of parenting the child receives. Remember one thing about ADHD if you don't remember anything else about the disorder. Children who suffer with the disorder are not taught how the disorder makes them act and have no control over their misbehaving.

**Myth #5: If You Weren't Diagnosed With The Disorder As A Child, You Can't Have It Once You Are An Adult - FALSE.** There are probably as many children or more that are misdiagnosed with the disorder and oftentimes go undiagnosed as well as the ones who are diagnosed with it.

**Myth #6: Diagnosing ADHD In Adults Is Literally Impossible - FALSE.** There is no single test used to diagnose adult ADHD. Both the American Medical Association and the Diagnostic and Statistical Manual of Mental Disorders offer documentation and a listing for Attention Deficit Hyperactivity Disorder in adults as well as children. This means that there are specific standards that are involved in the documentation of the disorder.

## Chapter 6: Anti-Social Butterfly

Sometimes things can seem shrouded in mist. While I believed that I was generally aware of what was going on, in the back of my mind I had a sneaking suspicion I was missing things. Take conversations for example. While I've had or heard just as many of them as everyone else, it can be difficult to follow along properly. This is most noticeable during personal interactions. "Zone-outs" make recalling the topic of conversation difficult, and formulating a proper response can be a mad scramble. As a result, people sometimes feel insulted because it seems as if I'm not listening to what they have to say. In the classroom, being perceived in this way creates disadvantage for students with ADHD because they may appear deliberately inattentive.

ADHD carries a tendency toward impulsiveness. From time to time I blurt out something completely inappropriate or unrelated to what is going on around me, or break out in fits of laughter over something that no one else understands. This caused a lot of misery for me during my high school years. I wasn't a fighter, but my behaviors that I was to be involved in more than my fair share. I discovered that sarcasm could be used as a shield against feeling out of place. Reactions to it generally fall into two classes: appreciation of the intelligence required to use it correctly, or anger at a perceived insult because the listener can't understand what's really being said. Unfortunately, most of my listeners fell into the second category. Most teenage boys aren't known for their grasp of higher-order wit or ability to handle insults amicably.

The end result can be a constant feeling that one is strange, out-of-place, disliked...pick your poison. Everyone knows how cruel kids and sometimes even teachers can be when someone who doesn't fit their idea of normal. When a sense of "differentness" is thrust upon you early, it can be hard to overcome both in your own mind and in the way others see you.

School Daze and Hyperfocus

ADHD sufferers inevitably experience problems issues with focus. We are easily distracted, making it difficult to form and follow through with plans and work in an organized fashion. These distractions may be **external**, such as when the sound of a plane passing overhead direction diverts your attention, or **internal** where disconnected thoughts, subjects, and half-formed plans bouncing uncontrollably in and out of the consciousness.

For me, internal distractions are the worst. It's like being caught in a thunderstorm. Lightning flashes of thought suddenly intrude which can't be ignored, followed by others that crash in like unanticipated thunderclaps. They instantly wipe out any sense of continuity, and as if this wasn't enough, the background is peppered with constant, rain-like pings. It's difficult to pinpoint their source, but they're always there ready to add the confusion. If reading my description of it seems hard to process, imagine how it feels when it's happening in **your** head.

The only way I am able to truly overcome this is through episodes of **hyperfocus**. In this state, my ability to concentrate is so complete that outside disruptions can't penetrate. Achieving it is easiest when I'm engaged in something stimulating enough to make me forget everything else. It's an incredible feeling, and unfortunately, I crave it so much that I actively seek it, and have even experimented in order to find it. Once I find something that puts me into a state of hyperfocus, I typically repeat the action over and over again. Eventually this became the basis of an addiction, although it was years before I realized it.

Many people operate under the misconception that people with ADHD are unintelligent while nothing could be further from the truth. In many cases, people with the condition have higher than average IQs. However, the symptoms of their disorder can mask the fact. While I was a slightly better-than-average student, I would certainly not have been labeled high-performing. Then, during my senior year, I took the American College Testing college readiness assessment (ACT) and scored 33 out of 36, placing me in the 99th percentile of high school seniors. This entitled me to a full scholarship to the college or university of my choice. It may have come as a surprise to my secondary school teachers, but it was enough to fool the university, and as a result, I was placed in several honors classes when I started college.

One of those classes was biology. With only one year of general science under my belt, I was lost from the first day. Not only could I not follow the lectures, but I posed a clear and present danger to myself and others in the lab. I sliced my finger while dissecting a sheep's eye, leaving a pool of blood in the dissection tray. I also managed to spill formaldehyde all over the place. No one died, but at least if they had, they'd have been well-preserved. I'm sure there were other events I can't remember, but I'm afraid of the possible dangers of relating the story. In any case, my performance left everything to be desired. My fellow students probably felt that Kevlar vests in order if they were to set foot in the lab safely.

Before the final exam, the professor and I had a one-on-one. "You realize that there's no way you can pass this class? No grade will bring your current average up far enough. I'm going to suggest that you not worry about this final and concentrate on some of your others."

"I'd like to take it anyway" I said.

"It's a waste of time," he warned, but he couldn't stop me from taking it.

I began studying at 6:00 the night before the exam. Around midnight, I suddenly hit my stride. I entered into some sort of zone where the only thing that existed was biology. I didn't hear the noise in the dorm. My roommate came in, took a shower, and got ready for bed, and I never noticed she was there. I worked all night long, reviewed the entire book, and was in class for the 8:00 exam.

Two days later, I was summoned to the professor's office where I was handed my test. "**An A?**" I asked with raised eyebrows. "An A," he confirmed. "Actually, it was the highest grade in the class." He looked at me curiously for a moment and said, "I don't believe you cheated, and the way the class is structured, if you found a way to cheat, you deserve an A." I explained to him how I had studied.

"You're not a science major of any sort, are you?"

"No."

"Will this class fulfill your science requirement?"

"Yes."

He stood up and stared out the window. "I'm going to give you a D- so you'll pass." Then he turned to look at me. "I'll pass you so that your science requirement is fulfilled, but **please** don't set foot in this building again."

I had **no** problem with that.

That marathon study session was my first experience with hyperfocus. I didn't know how I'd done it, or how it was fundamentally different from the rest of my study experiences, but I actively began trying to recreate it. Rather than struggling to keep up with daily study sessions, I ignored them. "Traditional" attendance and study methods increased my stress levels, so I started attending lectures **only to listen**. Being lessed stressed made it possible to absorb more of the material. The night before an exam would be spent cramming as much "learning" in as possible.

My grades improved a bit, but I still struggled to recreate the feeling I'd had while studying for the biology test. At some point during that session, I began to see connections I'd never seen before. It was as if I was able to see the whole of biology, and the answers became obvious as I learned to put things together. It was a powerful feeling... as if I could learn anything. I remember wondering if this was how other people felt all of the time. I began to alter my behavior in an attempt to recreate it. In retrospect, this may not have been a great idea.

## Chapter 7: Taking Charge Of Adhd

**W**e often advise parents not to worry so much about the label but to focus on proactive steps they can take to help their son. To raise a successful son with ADHD, you must start doing things differently from the day you find out your son's diagnosis.

Recognize That ADHD Is a Disability

Even though your son may look fine on the outside, his mind is wired very differently. Taking a "disability perspective" provides understanding. You are taking a great step by reading this book and teaching yourself more about ADHD as an increase in your knowledge about the condition is key to raising a successful son.

Try to Become More Understanding and Patient

That doesn't mean you will let your son "get away with things," but you will need to learn to respond differently. When Jim gets upset or frustrated with his son, he tends to point his index finger at Teddy and shake it up and down as he scolds him. Jim became so frustrated at himself and was determined to stop this automatic response. One day, he decided to write the letters "u" and "p" on the edge of his finger. When he got upset and pointed his finger at Teddy, Jim got an automatic visual reminder to have understanding and patience. This simple strategy worked!

Locate Support Personnel

Begin to locate different support personnel such as educators, counselors, and doctors who can serve as resources throughout the years. Part of raising a successful son with ADHD is recognizing that it's very tough to try to do it alone. If your son is going to be successful, at the very minimum, you must have his teachers' support.

Prepare for the Long Haul

It is important that you realize that you and your son are going to have really good periods and really rough patches and that meaningful change will occur over time. Remember that maturation helps most boys with ADHD, and as they move from the preschool to upper elementary years, the tantrums and tears tend to decrease.

ADHD Is Real

At times you still may wonder or have to convince a skeptical family member if ADHD is a fad or made-up disorder. Rest assured, ADHD is not a diagnosis contrived by parents or professionals looking for an excuse for a child's behavior.

The core symptoms of ADHD are developmentally inappropriate levels of inattention, hyperactivity, and impulsivity. In line with this, the National Resource Center on ADHD (2008) defined ADHD as "a condition affecting children and adults that is characterized by problems with attention, impulsivity, and over activity."

Most recent theories of ADHD have viewed behavioral inhibition as central to the disorder, while also suggesting that deficits in executive function and self-regulation are likely to account for part or all of the inattentive symptoms associated with the disorder.

These definitions have the following in common: ADHD is highly disruptive, involves too much energy or being too distracted, and is neurologically based. The behaviors must occur to a degree that is highly typical of children the same age and must interfere with academic or social progress. Finally, the behaviors must occur across multiple settings.

ADHD parenting is no easy task. Aside from making sure your child does well in school, does his or her chores, and stays out of trouble, you have keep your child safe from accidents. Although there is no official data to confirm this, those of us with ADHD kids have noticed they are more accident-prone than the average child.

The nature of the disorder increases the risks of these accidents. Kids and teens with ADHD are impulsive and easily distractible; their inability to think before they act or their lack of concentration makes them more susceptible to injury. The risk increases if the child has a language, motor, or learning disability, as many kids with ADHD do. If a child cannot follow what the teacher is saying or does not understand directions, the risk for accidents increases even more.

With a little supervision and vigilance, you can prevent the likelihood of injuries. Here's how you can keep your ADHD kids accident-free.

Young children (3-6 years)

Pre-school aged children are constantly on the go, even if they don't have ADHD. The difference is that the child with ADHD will climb too high, run too far, or cross the street without looking. Because of this, your ADHD child cannot play outdoors without adult supervision. Make sure your home is completely child-proofed; all kitchen cabinets and drawers must be locked, sharp table ends covered in rubber, and all breakable items out of reach. If your child has to be watched by a babysitter, make sure he or she is aware of your child's disorder and insist your child be supervised at all times.

Older children (6-12 years)

The same concerns for younger kids go for older ones as well, especially since older children are more active in outdoor activities and sports. They go skateboarding, swim in pools, or hiking, and they may have poorer judgment than their non-ADHD friends. This means adult supervision is a must. Another way of reducing injuries is by finding an ADHD treatment that works. Seek the advice of a health care specialist and work together to find interventions that will benefit your child.

Teens (13 and up)

The good news is you should be able to find ways to manage your child's ADHD symptoms throughout the years. This is important because as your ADHD child grows up, he or she will take on more responsibilities that increase the risk of accidents. For instance, ADHD kids who drive are more likely to experience road accidents because they get easily distracted, change lanes too quickly, or take needless driving risks.

Aside from that, teens with ADHD crave new stimuli more than those without ADHD; the likelihood that an ADHD teen will become sexually active, start smoking, or misuse alcohol or drugs is great. Fortunately, this can be prevented by keeping your child busy with healthy activities like sports or art classes. Make sure you do not stop ADHD treatments unless the doctor says otherwise.

Freedom and Impulse

Just because a child has ADHD doesn't make them "bad" kids; however, what it does make them is many times more impulsive. Unfortunately what happens is when a decision has to be made whether right or wrong, children with ADHD many times make quick choices and forget to consider the consequences of their actions until it's too late. Many times battles at school and at home become battles because the many people do not understand the actions of children with ADHD.

Children with ADHD become overwhelmed very easily when asked to do both abstract and too many tasks at the same time. They see things as black and white with no gray areas. They struggle with organization, problem solving and impulsiveness, so it's always wise that when you are aware of an ADHD child keep in mind they may in fact have some of the mentioned problems.

A child with ADHD often has trouble paying attention, inattention to details and makes careless mistakes, easily distracted, loses school supplies, forgets to turn in homework, trouble finishing class work and homework, trouble listening, trouble following multiple adult commands, blurts out answers, impatience fidgets or squirms, leaves their seat and runs about or climbs excessively, seems "on the go," talks too much and has difficulty playing quietly, interrupts or intrudes on others.

At home the child may show many of the same signs with the addition of some others. I see home behaviors many times increase because in the typical home most families are busy and have things to do in the evenings and weekends, thus making it unstructured and not a routine for the child. They become very overwhelmed just from the non-structure.

By being aware of their weaknesses, adults can be very instrumental in diverting a problem situation before it gets out of hand allowing not only the child with ADHD to keep their dignity but allowing the others to view the child with ADHD in a positive way and not always as the child getting into trouble. I have seen children with ADHD get frustrated over and over again because they are trying so hard to "be good" and no matter what they feel they can't. What we see is that eventually they just give up. When they get bad grade after bad grade when they are working and trying as hard as they can, eventually the helplessness takes over and they realize they can't do it anyway so why stress out.

Looking at the teens who are in trouble with the law, historically if we look back we can trace that most of these kids have problems that go back for years and moms report these children were many times difficult even while in the womb.

ADHD is not unique to the postmodern era. As early as 1845, a German physician wrote a poem about "Fidgety Philip," a boy who couldn't sit still at dinner and accidentally knocks all of the food onto the floor, to his parents' great displeasure. This is one of the earliest records of symptoms consistent with what we now call ADHD.

A great deal of research in the 1940s and 1950s focused on disorders of the brain. Scientists described ADHD-like behavior with terms such as "minimal brain dysfunction" or "hyperkinetic impulse disorder." In 1987, the third edition of the Diagnostic and Statistical Manual of Mental Disorders recognized the disorder as Attention Deficit Hyperactivity Disorder. Therefore, the notion that ADHD is a disorder made up in the 1990s is a myth.

## Chapter 8: The Causes

The jury is still out on the exact cause – or causes – of ADHD, but there seem to be several common themes coming through strongly. If you are a parent of a child who suffers from ADHD, it can be very distressing to be blamed for the bad behavior your child may display because of this condition. One thing that cannot be attributed to causing it is bad parenting, or not disciplining the child. So let's try and dismiss that unhelpful theory straightaway.

What is it?

It used to be considered that diet was a high contributory factor but this has lost some credence recently. Rather, it is caused by chemical imbalances or abnormalities in the brain. In a child some or all of the following symptoms will be present:

●Restlessness – not being able to sit still

●Lack of concentration

- Forgetfulness

- Running round or climbing on things with no perception of danger

- Shouting things out in class – unable to contain themselves and interrupts others

- Seems like they're not listening

- Talkative

Obviously, these symptoms are bad enough for a child. Their schoolwork suffers and their ability to make friendships with their peers and so they do not get a chance to become socialized. Inexperienced professionals may not fully understand the disorder and so the child receives inappropriate discipline.

Left untreated, this can lead to more serious problems in the teenage years and adulthood. Teenagers suffering from ADHD may get into trouble at school or with the police. The common complaint from a teenager that his parent does not understand him is probably true in their case. They may turn to illegal drugs and develop addictions and of course, their academic achievements can be poorer because of lack of concentration of an inability to see things through to the end.

As the sufferer grows into an adult, problems can worsen and lead to anxiety because of the related problems the condition brings with it. There is a multitude of symptoms such as:

- Depression – a feeling of being unable to cope

- Anxiety – worrying about being able to complete or finish something

- Relationship problems

- Moodiness

- Substance abuse – sometimes leading to addiction

- Lack of concentration – cannot read or perform tasks at work

- Quick to anger and frustration

- Acting on impulse

- Lack of self confidence – so many past failures

- Acting on impulse

- Recklessness, no sense of danger

- Can't stop talking

## Causes

So if we have ruled out what does not cause ADHD, what does cause it?

## Genetics

There is now strong evidence – a 50% chance - that this condition can be passed down from parent to child through the genes. It is also likely that if one child suffers there is a 30% chance of a sibling doing so also.

## Pregnancy Problems

If a woman smokes or drinks during pregnancy, this can have an adverse effect on the unborn child's brain development.

## Food additives

There seems to be a weak link between food additives and ADHD, but the FDA says that this link is tenuous at best and additives are not harmful to children. Nevertheless, it is likely that additives and food colorings will affect a small number of children. It is becoming increasingly common to find how harmful additives or substitutes can be. Why take a chance when you can prepare natural food yourself and know exactly what went into it? This can be done as a family and encourage the joy of cooking in your child.

Food allergies

The medical consensus is that food plays only a small part in ADHD. Nevertheless, it cannot be entirely ruled out to be a cause for some because everyone's genetic and physical makeup is unique. A high number of children can be allergic to various foodstuffs and this can precipitate various symptoms on a spectrum of severity. One of these can be ADHD. Fortunately, many children become immune to the allergy over time whilst others continue to suffer from the allergy, which makes ADHD symptoms worse. Food allergies can be detected with a simple blood test, but this can prove costly and is unlikely to be offered easily if the symptoms are not severe or producing physical signs such as shortage of breath, swelling or rashes. Some common culprits of food allergens can be wheat found in bread or cookies, dairy products including eggs and milk and sadly chocolate, fish and shellfish. It can be established if any of these foods are causing an allergy by eliminating them from the diet one at a time to see if symptoms decrease but consult your doctor before doing this.

In the next chapter we will go on to discuss traditional treatment, i.e., drugs, and what risk that carries, if any. By choosing this book, you have probably already decided to look for more natural ways to treat ADHD but is this necessary or helpful?

## Chapter 9: Getting Your Facts Straight

With all that is seen in the media about ADHD, many people picture a naughty and destructive boy. And they often think they could spot a person with ADHD if they were to come across them. Well, in some cases they may get it right. But even a broken clock tells the right time twice a day!

But in some cases, it could be a child who is quiet and refuses to leave her mothers' side. It maybe the teenager who has communication problems, is very polite but says little to nothing most days. In the majority of cases the average person would have difficulty in spotting someone with ADHD

But there are some common symptoms that are easy to spot. Those who live with this disorder may suffer from forgetfulness, distraction, is highly disorganized, cannot keep up with a fast conversation and may suffer from low self esteem.

Common symptoms may also include:

A lack of vigor

Places more value on others than themselves

Will not assert them selves

Very obedient

Can be very modest

Very polite

Very shy

Prefers to stay away from crowds, socially withdrawn

Girls are often overlooked

Because many people believe that little girls are normally quieter than little boys, then they will suffer in silence with ADHD and go undiagnosed. ADHD girls can be very sensitive to the slightest criticism and highly emotional. As they get older, they will avoid stressful situations and will keep to themselves with feelings of very low self esteem.

How to help those with ADHD

Those with ADHD will often come into contact with others who don't realize that they have the disorder. This may lead to them being overly criticized at school or at work. We all have to face both fair and unfair criticism during our normal routines. But those with ADHD have difficulty with criticism and stressful situations.

So the best thing you can do to help is simply to try and create a calmer environment for them and cut right back with any unnecessary criticism. There are always methods to get your point across without being critical.

Criticism is something that can't be cut out altogether so it is also worth showing them how to deal with criticism when it is constructive, and criticism when it is unfair. These are skills that we may take for granted but those with ADHD very often do not know how to deal with it.

You can't control the environment at school or work for them but you can make a difference at home. This is a place where they can return to, get themselves revitalized and ready for another day.

Finding the chance to compliment

Life in the real world can be hard for those with ADHD. Their confidence can take a battering during the day and they will often feel low and in severe cases, worthless. Sometimes, it just takes the right words to turn this around. This is where giving a compliment will help.

We all love to receive a compliment. Those who suffer with ADHD are exactly the same. Giving a compliment at the right time can restore some self worth. It can be a compliment on anything from their smile, their manners, their actions or anything else. Being quick to compliment and slow to criticize is a great philosophy to have and it will be a much needed boost to their esteem.

## Chapter 10: Adhd In The Home

Often your child's behavior will not only be affecting your relationship with him, but also the relationship he has with other members of the family. Because the child with ADHD will often demand attention even when you are dealing with something or someone else, this will leave less time for interaction with other family members. He will cut into your conversations with his brothers and sisters no matter how important they might be or how often you ask him not to. He might leave messes that he forgets to clean up or stay up late at night and disturb the sleep of siblings. Children with ADHD often say inappropriate things that might embarrass or hurt the feelings of other members of the family. As a result of these things brothers and sisters and other relatives can become very resentful of the child with ADHD. Jealousy can set in when they think he is getting all the attention and they might even say and do things to hurt the child's feelings or refuse to spend time with him. Remember that the other children and sometimes even adults in the home also need your attention. Enlist their help when engaging in activities with your ADHD child. When rewarding the child with ADHD always remember to give the other family members positive reinforcement as well.

The child with ADHD wants to do the right thing but he cannot do it on his own. He wants to maintain order and follow instruction but you need to help him. There are several ways that the parents of children with ADHD can help their children to control the symptoms of the disorder.

· Help your child by channeling all that energy into areas that are productive such as chores or sports and other types of physical activity. Find ways of learning that are fun and exciting.

·Help your child by showing him how to make friends with other children. Arrange for play or set up playtime with relatives who are roughly of the same age. Sports and games can also be an avenue for social interaction with other children.

· Give structure to your child's life by establishing rules and boundaries. If a child with ADHD lives in an environment that is disorganized and in chaos, his behavior will worsen so it is important to have a structured and organized home. Discipline and order must have a place in the home.

· Help your child to set reachable and realistic goals. It is often said that if you don't know where you are going you have no way of knowing when you get there. So chart a path for your child and know exactly where you want that path to take you. You must have an idea of what your child is capable of. Try to ensure that he reaches his full potential.

## Chapter 11: How Is Adults Diagnosed With Adhd?

It's important to talk to your doctor or a psychiatrist to assess whether symptoms merit a diagnosis of ADHD. Many adults may struggle with focusing or time management at different points in life, but to receive a diagnosis of ADHD, symptoms have to cause continual problems at work, home, or relationships.

A professional can also rule out other physical or mental illnesses or consider additional diagnoses which can complicate symptoms. These might include bipolar disorder, depression, anxiety disorders, learning disabilities, or substance use problems.

Common questions asked by your physician might include:

Do you ever have trouble with paying attention or feeling restless?

Do you easily become frustrated or impatient with minor issues?

Do you have trouble organizing tasks or following through with them at work?

Does lack of time management or focus cause problems in your relationships?

Did you have problems with inattentiveness or hyperactivity as a child?

Does anyone in your family have a diagnosis of ADHD?

Do you have any other medical or mental health issues?

Treatment Options for Adult ADHD

Treatment for Adult ADHD typically involves medication, psychotherapy, and/or psych education. There is no cure for ADHD, but a combination of these treatments can effectively reduce symptoms and improve work and home life.

Medication treatments can include stimulants, nonstimulants, or antidepressants. Stimulants can work more quickly than other medication, but they also can be habit-forming. Be sure to talk to your doctor about other medications you're taking and if you have a history of substance use.

Psychotherapy for Adult ADHD typically involves a combination of talk therapy and psychoeducation. Cognitive behavioral therapy can help a person reduce negative thinking, increase self-esteem, and adjust behavioral patterns that cause problems at work or home.

Family therapy can help people work together to manage the stress of ADHD and practice problem-solving. Basic psych education can include information about the diagnosis and healthy living skills, such as time management, problem-solving, and communication skills

ADHD IN CHILDREN

Attention deficit hyperactivity disorder (ADHD) is neurodevelopmental condition that develops when the brain and central nervous system suffer impairments related to growth and development.

A child with attention deficit hyperactivity disorder (ADHD) may struggle throughout the day to maintain their attention. He or she may appear restless and engage in hyperactive or impulsive behaviors.

For kids, ADHD can interfere with their school work, their relationships with other people, and how they view themselves in the world. These symptoms can persist into adulthood, causing work and relationship problems.

Symptoms have been detected in children as young as 3, and they typically start before the age of 12. ADHD is more common among boys than girls, and the symptoms can be mild, moderate, or severe.

The condition may also manifest differently depending on the individual. Some people experience mainly symptoms of inattention, which is known as the predominantly inattentive subtype of ADHD. The predominantly hyperactive-impulsive subtype describes individuals who mainly experience symptoms of hyperactivity and impulsivity. Finally, most people with ADHD experience a combination of all symptoms and fall under the combined subtype.

What does inattention look like?

Inattention symptoms can look different depending on the situation, but common symptoms in children include:

being easily distracted.

forgetting to do chores, disliking homework, losing items or assignments.

struggling to follow instructions and have trouble paying attention to details.

difficulty following through with tasks or with managing their time.

easily frustrated with difficult tasks; trouble coping with stressful situations.

Parents and teachers might feel like a child isn't listening to them even when they are speaking to them.

What do hyperactivity and impulsivity look like?

Although all children may be impulsive or hyperactive at certain times, a child who is hyperactive and impulsive will frequently:

fidget or squirm when trying to be still. They may have trouble staying in their seat in class, or run around and climb on or under things.

find it difficult to participate quietly in activities, often talking too much, interrupting others, or blurting out answers when it's not their turn.

How does a child get diagnosed with ADHD?

A child needs to have experienced symptoms for at least 6 months, and these symptoms must disrupt life in multiple settings. For example, a child's inattention and/or hyperactivity would be causing problems both at home and school.

The symptoms also must not match behavior for most children in their age group. For example, all 3-year-olds have short attention spans and can be very energetic at times.

It's also important to remember that all children are different. Just because one child is more animated than a sibling does not mean they have ADHD.

What challenges does a child with ADHD experience?

ADHD poses unique challenges for young people. These can include trouble with academic work or negative stereotypes that teachers and other students may express about ADHD. They also may experience poor self-image as they struggle to master tasks at home and school.

A child with ADHD is also at risk for accident and injury due to inattention and impulsivity. As a child with ADHD becomes older, they may also be at risk for experimenting with drug and alcohol use and other risky behaviors.

What will happen when we see a doctor?

Your family doctor or your child's pediatrician is an excellent first stop for evaluating and treating possible ADHD. They may choose to refer you to a clinician who specializes in the condition or to an evaluator for future assessment. They may also recommend coordination with school counselors and psychologists to tailor your child's behavioral and educational plan in a way that serves them best.

A clinician will also rule out other causes of symptoms, which can include conditions such as anxiety, depression, oppositional defiant disorder, learning disabilities, conduct disorder, etc.

While there is no cure for ADHD, symptoms can be managed with the right treatment and support team. Treatment for ADHD typically includes medication to help reduce symptoms, and cognitive behavioral therapy which teaches coping skills for day-t0-day challenges.

Starting treatment early can have a huge impact in the life and self-esteem of a child. With a combination of medication and/or self-management techniques, children can learn to build the life skills necessary to thrive in school, build healthy relationships, and foster a positive self-image that will serve them well into adulthood. Consider what steps you can take today to help your child build a healthy and happy future.

## Chapter 12: Ginseng As An Adhd Treatment Option

Ginseng is well-regarded for its memory boosting, sleep improving, and brain-saving longevity benefits. In a general sense, it appears that it would be a good potential treatment method for ADHD and related disorders. Although successful clinical study publications on the specific use of ginseng for ADHD are relatively scarce, it appears that on at least a theoretical basis, this popular herb could work for treating ADHD and related disorders. I would like to highlight some of the biochemical and physiological reasons supporting its use as an alternative treatment for ADHD:

Compound diversity in ginseng: Ginseng is not simply one isolated compound, such as an individual drug, but rather a mixture of substances of potential pharmaceutical benefit. Among these are a family of compounds called ginsenosides. One of the underlying benefits this (and herbal treatments in general), is that many of these related compounds can work together in a synergistic fashion, nature's own alternative to drug cocktails. Given the fact that absorption, metabolism and utilization of biochemical agents for the treatment of disorders is rarely due to one isolated substance of pharmaceutical value, this multi-compound treatment method certainly has potential advantages over a single-drug treatment method for ADHD or related disorders.

Ginseng, dopaminergic activity, and ADHD: It has been demonstrated that herbal extracts of ginseng can exhibit activities that target the dopaminergic (dopamine-related) pathway and can exhibit neuro-protective benefits for these pathways. This is important, because ADHD is often chemically characterized by deficits in this pathway, which typically include reduced dopamine levels in the regions between neuronal cells throughout various key regions of the brain (ones that, among other things, are responsible for attention span, screening out irrelevant stimuli, and impulse control). There are even implications that ginseng compounds can accelerate the neurodevelopment process from stem cells.

Boosting of "synaptic plasticity": During the learning process, a certain amount of "agility" is necessary in the regions in between the cells as the brain begins to rewire itself to conform to the newly learned material. The ability of neurons to form new connections is referred to as synaptic plasticity. It appears that ginseng contains several key elements which helps maintain this "pliable" learning-friendly state. Essentially, compounds isolated from ginseng can moderate long-term potentiation, (long term potentiation refers to a learning and memory process in which communication between two neuronal cells is improved or made more efficient by stimulating both cells at the same time. This plays an important role in the development and maintenance of long-term memories). Given the fact that learning disabilities are frequently seen in ADHD (often more on the inattentive side of the ADHD spectrum), it stands to reason that ginseng may be useful in some of these comorbid learning-related deficits as well.

Ginseng boosts aerobic glucose metabolism in the ADHD brain: The ADHD brain typically contains deficits of glucose and oxygen (as determined by multiple imaging and brain scanning studies) in many of the key brain regions which modulate attentional control, impulsivity, and concentration. It is even postulated that ADHD may be an "energy deficient syndrome". Brain metabolic studies indicate that aerobic glucose metabolism is typically improved in the presence of ginseng isolates. Not only does this reduce some of the potentially brain waste products associated with oxygen-deprived brain activity, but this enhanced aerobic form of glucose metabolism in the brain is a more efficient process.

Ginseng may boost dopamine and norepinephrine levels: As mentioned previously, individuals with ADHD are typically deficient of the important neuro-signaling agent dopamine in key regions of the brain. However, a deficiency in another important neuro-signaling agent called norepinephrine is also frequently seen in the ADHD brain. Imbalances of both dopamine and norepinephrine are seen in ADHD patients, and can lead to disruptions in physiological processes such as attention span, complex cognitive processes, auditory processing delays, and motor behavioral dysfunctions. It is believed that the ginsenoside compounds (see point #1) may help alleviate some of these ADHD-related symptoms by boosting levels of dopamine and norepinephrine in these key brain regions, several of which are affiliated with ADHD.

Interestingly, many stimulant meds for ADHD work by boosting levels of these same two compounds, meaning the effects of ginseng may approximate those of a stimulant medication used to treat ADHD. We will see in the next post how another natural brain supplement, Ginkgo biloba, may better approximate the action of non-stimulant ADHD medications. It is also worth noting that isolates of ginseng and ginkgo may work in tandem to boost memory and other related functions.

On a side note, fatty extracts of the ginseng plant have been used to alleviate the dopamine-dependent "high" of cocaine, which supports the use of ginseng as a potential treatment agent for cocaine addictions. Similar results support the use of ginseng for treating nicotine addiction as well. This further validates the dopamine-dependent regulatory benefits of ginseng and its ability to stabilize fluctuations in neuro-signaling agents of relevance to ADHD.

Ginseng may protect against brain damage from excess iron: I have personally advocated the use of iron for treating ADHD in several other posts. It can counteract toxic effects of lead and other metals, improve the synthesis of dopamine from the dietary amino acid tyrosine, and improve sleep quality in ADHD children. However, there are several dangers associated with excessive iron supplementation, one of which is neuronal death and neuro-degenerative diseases such as Parkinson's. However, there is some evidence that ginseng can counteract this iron-related neuronal damage by regulating specific iron-transporting proteins in the brain. If these findings hold true, then ginseng might be of use as some type of "insurance measure" against potential damage from excessive amounts of iron supplementation designed to treat ADHD.

Promote nerve growth in brain regions typically under-developed in ADHD: We have reported earlier on some of the delays in maturation and development of specific brain regions in ADHD. Some research suggests that ginseng compounds may promote neuronal growth and development in the early stages of life. While currently a bit of a stretch, findings such as this may lead to the use of ginseng compounds to offset ADHD-associated neurodevelopmental delays somewhere down the road.

Neuroprotective effects of ginseng for the aging ADHD brain: This may be especially relevant to adults with ADHD as they age. In addition to its ability to help with neuronal cell development in the early stages of life (mentioned in the previous point), evidence suggests that the active ginsenoside "Rd" compound in ginseng can alleviate inflammatory damage and death to neuronal cells. Given the fact that early neurodegenerative effects are often present in ADHD-like mammalian systems, these results at least suggest that ginseng may be a potential life-long treatment option for individuals diagnosed with ADHD.

## How to Take It

### Pediatric

This herb is not recommended for use in children because of its stimulant properties.

### Adult

Dried root: 500 to 2000 mg daily (can be purchased in 250 mg capsules).

Tea/infusion: Pour 1 cup boiling water over 1 tsp finely chopped ginseng root. Steep for 5 to 10 minutes. Prepare and drink one to three times daily for three or four weeks.

Tincture (1:5): 1 to 2 teaspoons

Liquid extract (1:1): ¼ to ½ teaspoon

Standardized extract (4% total ginsenosides): 100 mg twice daily

In healthy individuals who wish to increase physical or mental performance, to prevent illness, or to improve resistance to stress, ginseng should be taken in one of the above dosages for two to three weeks, followed by a break of two weeks.

For help recovering from an illness, the elderly should take 500 mg twice daily for three months. Alternatively, they may take the same dosage (500 mg twice daily) for a month, followed by a two-month break. This can then be repeated if desired.

Precautions

The use of herbs is a time-honored approach to strengthening the body and treating disease. Herbs, however, contain active substances that can trigger side effects and interact with other herbs, supplements, or medications. For these reasons, herbs should be taken with care, under the supervision of a practitioner knowledgeable in the field of botanical medicine.

Both American and Asian ginsengs are stimulants and may cause nervousness or sleeplessness, particularly if taken at high doses. Other reported side effects include high blood pressure, insomnia, restlessness, anxiety, euphoria, diarrhea, vomiting, headache, nosebleed, breast pain, and vaginal bleeding. To avoid hypoglycemia (low blood sugar), even in non-diabetics, ginseng should be taken with food.

The American Herbal Products Association (AHPA) rates ginseng as a class 2d herb, which indicates that specific restrictions apply. In this case, hypertension (high blood pressure) is the specific restriction. People with hypertension should not take ginseng products without specific guidance and instruction from a qualified practitioner. At the same time, people with low blood pressure as well as those with an acute illness or diabetes (because of the risk of a sudden drop in blood sugar), should use caution when taking ginseng.

Safety of taking ginseng during pregnancy is unknown; therefore, it is not recommended when pregnant or breast feeding.

Ginseng should be discontinued at least 7 days prior to surgery. This is for two reasons. First, ginseng can lower blood glucose levels and, therefore, create problems for patients fasting prior to surgery. Also, ginseng may act as a blood thinner, thereby increasing the risk of bleeding during or after the procedure.

Possible Interactions

If you are currently being treated with any of the following medications, you should not use ginseng without first talking to your healthcare provider:

Blood Thinning Medications

There have been reports that ginseng may possibly decrease the effectiveness of the blood-thinning medication, warfarin. In addition, ginseng may inhibit platelet activity and, therefore, should probably not be used with aspirin either.

Caffeine

While taking ginseng, it is wise to avoid caffeine or other substances that stimulate the central nervous system because the ginseng may increase their effects, possibly causing nervousness, sweating, insomnia, or irregular heartbeat.

Ginseng and Haloperidol

Ginseng may exaggerate the effects of this anti-psychotic medication, so they should not be taken together.

Morphine

Ginseng may block the pain killing effects of morphine.

Phenelzine and other MAOIs for Depression

There have been reports of a possible interaction between ginseng and the antidepressant medication, phenelzine (which belongs to a class known as monoamine oxidase inhibitors [MAOIs]), resulting in symptoms ranging from manic-like episodes to headache and tremulousness.

## Chapter 13: Adhd And Emotions

It's no mystery at this point that emotional regulation is a serious concern for children and adults who struggle with ADHD. Often, people who suffer from this condition find themselves quick to anger and their anger tends to be dramatically disproportionate to the situation that caused it. This anger tends to stem from frustration and impatience. Besides, poor attention span can easily lead to a high level of impatience. People who suffer from ADHD may just not have it in them to listen to a lengthy explanation or wait for their turn with a toy or device. This impatience leads to frustration (sometimes with themselves and sometimes with you). Unless properly tempered, the end result can easily become a dramatic temper-tantrum.

Unfortunately, handling this issue is not as easy as simply teaching your child to have more patience. While patience is a positive virtue to reinforce, if it were that easy, than ADHD would become a largely curable condition. The truth is, these frustrations will occur. What you can do is model how to appropriately and effectively handle a situation. Your example is key. This is how your child will learn productive coping mechanisms that can help stop the tantrums before they start.

First and foremost, don't forget those strategies that we've already discussed. Good nutrition, plenty of sleep, and an established routine can all go a long way toward preventing outbursts. A child that is healthy and knows what to expect in their day is a child who will be less frustrated by changes in activity.

Next, teach your child to practice forgiveness. This may also be referred to as productive thinking. Basically, whether your child is frustrated with themselves or with something else, productive thinking will help them refocus their anger into something more solution oriented. In other words, if your son is upset because the rain is preventing him from riding his bike, take some time to find a solution with him. Maybe you can work together to reschedule a time for the bike ride. You could also work with him to think up some fun rainy day activities to do instead. In this way, your son learns to forgive the situation (or whomever he may be angry with).

If you notice a tantrum coming on, you may need to intervene with some more active and less cognitive coping mechanisms. For example, counting backward from ten with your child while you practice deep breathing can help bring them back to a place where they are ready to discuss solutions. You might also try something even more active to distract them from the tantrum, like having them do five jumping jacks or spin in a circle. Pay attention to your child's unique personality when figuring out what works. You should also take the time to discuss these strategies with them ahead of time. Make a deal with them that requires them to try some of these with you when they feel a tantrum coming on.

While it is always beneficial to stay involved in your child's life and be an active participant in their development, it is equally as important that they learn self-soothing strategies. After all, your child may be taking their ADHD into adulthood and they won't always have mom or dad there to count down from ten with them. Discuss these strategies with your child the same way you would discuss them with others. Let them tell you what they think would work and what wouldn't. Then, make a deal that your child will try one of these strategies when a tantrum is imminent. Self-soothing strategies could include listening to music, taking a bath, going for a run, reading, or even just sitting quietly and having a healthy snack.

Some therapeutic tools such as a card game known as Mad Dragon can help teach children how to regulate their emotions, develop self-soothing strategies, and verbally express their needs. Kade and I play Mad Dragon for this very reason and have seen enormous success from it. Playing a lot like Uno but using cards that ask kids if they make good choices when they're upset or instruct them to identify two healthy anger management strategies, Mad Dragon is incredibly effective.

No matter what strategies you choose to employ, the number one thing you can do to help your child learn effective anger management strategies is to lead by example. After all, you can't very well expect your child to learn about healthy ways to manage their emotions if you can't manage your own. What's more, using some of the techniques that you've discussed with your child when your own anger is coming on will help them see that these strategies are effective and may encourage them to employ them more earnestly.

# Chapter 14: Characteristics

Sometimes parents and other caregivers who work with young ones with learning disabilities may think the child is just lazy, spoiled, daydreaming, bored or is not disciplined.

Some of the most common characteristics are as follows:

Short attention span/easily distracted

Poor memory/forgetful

Difficulty following directions

Poor reasoning ability

Inability to set realistic goals

Poor reading ability (e.g., adds, omits, skips words when reading)

Difficulty distinguishing between p, g, b, d, and q

Reads "on" for "no", "was" for "saw", etc.

Difficulty with concepts left-right, above-below, up-down, yesterday-tomorrow, in-out, etc.

Difficulty telling time

Difficulty writing

Poor eye-hand coordination

Clumsy/accident prone

Disorganized/loses things

Quick tempered/easily irritated

Impulsive

Gets caught up in details

Childish and bossy behavior

Needs constant recognition

A loner

Some of these children are also very bright and can read very well. When it comes to writing this is a big problem for most of them, their writing is very sloppy and they themselves cannot understand it.

Lucky for computers some children can even do their work using computers instead of writing which makes it easier on the child and also for the caregivers.

Can Other Problems Be Mistaken For ADHD

Many children have mistakenly been diagnosed as having ADHD because there are several health problems that mimic some of the same signs and symptoms.

There is no test for making a diagnosis of ADHD. Tests are based on using standard guidelines from the American Academy of Pediatrics. A diagnosis is made by gathering information from the child parents or caregiver.

A child has to show some or all the symptoms on a regular basis for at least 6 months in 2 or more settings such as at school and at home. Both the parents and teacher or caregivers are asked to complete the questioners about the child's behavior and environment.

Many pediatricians will refer the child to see a mental health specialist who is experienced in childhood disorders. The doctors will try to rule out any other possibilities that may have these symptoms.

Physical and medical history.

A physical is taken to screen for visual or hearing problems, allergies, seizures and eczema which can all produce symptoms that mimic ADHD. You may have to ask your doctor to perform these tests some of them will but some of them would not.

There are also other conditions that can affect a child's behavior such as:

Mood disorders

Thyroid disorders

Anxiety disorders

Lead toxicity

Sleep dysfunction

Parasites

Chemical imbalance

When a child is diagnosed with ADHD there are normally other health problems that exist including:

Tourettes Syndrome

Learning disorders

Behavioral issues

Oppositional defiant disorder (ODD)

Anxiety

Depression

So a child with ADHD may have more to deal with other than just the ADHD.

Learning Disability

Alfred A. Strauss, M.D. is the first person to describe the behaviors of children and adults now identified as learning disability. These adults and children are not mentally retarded but some of them are very intelligent.

An individual with learning disability, the message to the brain becomes jumbled which makes it difficult for the individual to learn in one or more academic area. Despite this problem some of these individuals become very successful.

Some of these individuals who had learning disabilities were Thomas Edison, Albert Einstein, Nelson Rockefeller, Winston Churchill and many others. Many of them found a different approach to learning from how most people learn. Research shows that individuals with learning disabilities that go undetected do not do well in school.

The National Center for Learning Disabilities (http://www.ncld.org/) lists some words commonly associated with learning disabilities that will be helpful as you work with youth with learning disabilities.

Dyslexia, perhaps the most commonly known, is primarily used to describe difficulty with language processing and its impact on reading, writing, and spelling.

Dysgraphia involves difficulty with writing. Problems might be seen in the actual motor patterns used in writing. Also characteristic are difficulties with spelling and the formulation of written composition.

Dyscalculia involves difficulty with math skills and impacts math computation. Memory of math facts, concepts of time, money, and musical concepts can also be impacted.

Dyspraxia (Apraxia) is a difficulty with motor planning, and impacts upon a person's ability to coordinate appropriate body movements.

Auditory Discrimination is a key component of efficient language use, and is necessary to "break the code" for reading. It involves being able to perceive the differences between speech sounds, and to sequence these sounds into meaningful words.

Visual Perception is critical to the reading and writing processes as it addresses the ability to notice important details and assign meaning to what is seen.

Attention Deficit (Hyperactivity) Disorder (ADD/ADHD) may co-occur with learning disabilities (incidence estimates vary). Features can include: marked over-activity, distractibility, and/or impulsivity which in turn can interfere with an individual's availability to benefit from instruction.

## Chapter 15: Signs And Symptoms

Diagnosis is tough in the event of ADD because signs change from child to child. The signs and symptoms from the disorder might be apparent.

To begin with you've got to be obvious that simply since your child is hyperactive, he isn't struggling with ADD. It is a fact which more than normal activities are an indication of ADD although not always so.

But, simultaneously impulsive behavior, or under normal attention, or even more than usual distraction is an indication of ADD.

Really, distraction and insufficient attention match. An ADD suffering child won't have the ability to stay with his work and won't pay much focus on particulars and could not complete his work. Although most kids are just like this but individuals who are suffering from ADD show more extremes of the behavior can embark upon in excess of 6 several weeks. Thus his daily jobs are affected.

Kids getting ADD are impulsive too. They might all of a sudden try to escape using their desks to determine what's happening within the other area of the room. They might even hand out solutions within the class even when they aren't requested. His behavior might be impulsive to such extremes. It's a common trait in most ADD affected children.

These kids attach themselves to everything that's happening. They might become oversensitive and could not have the ability to focus on anything particularly. Hence their grades are less than usual even when it normally won't genuinely have difficulties in mastering anything simply because they don't complete their tasks. Their attention span is really short that they're not capable of finishing the job allocated for them.

There's improvement in behavior one of the two sexes also. Boys tend to be more active and women are less mindful within the class. It is not easy to handle each of them and both might be unmanageable in behavior or aggressive and might be even abusive. As a result it becomes tough to control them.

But all kids vary from one another. You won't ever find two similar kids. Only since your child is much more aggressive than the others don't jump towards the conclusion he has ADD. Merely a physician or perhaps a specialist can diagnose ADD.

## Chapter 16: Supporting Students With Add/Adhd

Despite many challenges, ADHD will bring success to one's life. With good academic and life skills combined with hard work and perseverance a student will excel in their chosen field.

To ensure that a student has a productive life, it is important for parents and teachers to work together. Below are few simple steps you may want to consider when it comes to dealing with students with ADD/ADHD. Let this be a simple guide in making sure that your student or child will succeed.

Step 1: Communicate with the school personnel.

You should always communicate with the teachers, principal and other school personnel regarding your knowledge of your child's strengths and areas of improvement. Keep your child informed of these communications and actively ask for his or her input.  This will help build their self-esteem.    Teachers    are    trained professionals and they also value parent input and participation in educating the student.  They  are  professionals  and certainly know how to approach a student with  ADD/ADHD.  By  having  regular communications with your child's teacher you can help guide your child in preparing an  excellent  schedule  to  meet  their specific needs.  Keep in mind that the plan and  schedule  will  change  with  the development of the student.  That is to be expected.  It is very important to start the plan as soon as possible.

Step 2: Develop a Plan for your Children

A Plan will have a list of action steps for managing a student's academic and social goals.    Several    factors    are    usually considered in preparing good plan, these include the environment and peers your child socializes with, their academic goals and tasks.  Teachers can provide feedback for this document and help reinforce the academic goals at school.   This plan will allow the student to have a blue print for success. This will also help student with ADD/ADHD manage his daily routine and complete the daily tasks with greater ease.

Step 3: Prepare an environment that will allow them to concentrate and focus.

As mentioned earlier, focus is a very difficult task for a student with ADD/ADHD. In coordination with the teacher, work hard to make school fun and enjoyable for the students. Provide as much physical activities as possible. Also, place the student's seat away from the windows to avoid distractions.

Step 4: Provide structure to the student's life.

Students diagnosed with ADHD benefit from a lot of structure. Provide a routine for the student with a list of tasks. Coordinate the list with various colors. A color key will help student differentiate the tasks at hand and stay focused.

Patience is a virtue when it comes to helping students with ADHD succeed.

Many students need to have something in their hands to do. This may help some students focus better. Teacher and parent should monitor to ensure that this object does not become a toy. Stress balls and loose rubber bands around hand may also help.

One Focal Point

Depending of task at hand, having a focal point may be a challenge but can be worked toward. Each student is different so teachers and parents need to monitor and analyze to see what works best for the individual student. Sometimes doodling during parent and teacher instruction may be permitted. This helps the student focus. Elaborate pictures take away from focus.

Frequent breaks are highly recommended. Students should take breaks with knowledge that they will get back to the task at hand.

## Chapter 17: Adhd And The Whole Family: What You Need To Know And Do?

Living with a child who has ADHD (Attention Deficit Hyperactivity Disorder) can be frustrating and sometimes overwhelming, as well; but as parents, there are things that you can do to help your child lessen and control the symptoms of the said condition. Children with ADHD are hyperactive, and they usually act without thinking. They also have difficulties focusing. They may understand and may be aware of the things that their family or teachers expected from them, but they have trouble obeying or following everything to the dot because they can't attend to details, pay attention, or even sit still.

Parents can help their children with ADHD get through the day without so much trouble, and to overcome the seemingly impossible tasks that they need to do or accomplish. Parents can also help their children channel their vigor doing positive things and bring ease to the entire family. It is prudent to address the problems at the nearest possible time, and allow the children with ADHD to gain greater chances to succeed.

What Anyone Needs to Know?

The entire family must understand that children with ADHD don't have the ability to organize things, complete tasks, control their impulses, make critical analysis, and plan in advance. This only indicates that the parents (and anyone in the family) need to provide extra guidance, and allow the children to slowly acquire the skills all on their own. You need to teach them how to do things, and expect such act to eat up a lot of your time and patience until they are able to do things right.

Maddening might not even be enough to describe the feeling when dealing with a child with ADHD, but you and your entire family need to have patience, and understand that the child is not doing things to embarrass or annoy everyone in the household willfully. Children with such condition prefer to sit quietly, want to keep their surroundings clean and well-organized, and do what their parents tell them to do, but the trouble is that they don't know how to make all of the mentioned things even possible.

Sufferers of ADHD are as frustrated as the people around them and they don't know how to openly state their frustrations. Perhaps, some of their actions are manifestations of frustrations regarding the feeling that they can't properly convey.  If you or anyone in the family will keep such fact in mind, then it will be a lot easier to be supportive. You can easily and positively respond to the needs of the child. Give your child a lot of love because doing so can make you more patient, supportive, and compassionate. Everyone in the household will also find enjoyment in sharing an unwavering and cheerful home together.

ADHD and the Entire Family

Before you can parent a child with ADHD without so much trouble, there is a need to fully understand the impact of the condition on the whole family, especially your other children. It is crucial not to make the siblings of an ADHD sufferer feel like they don't bear any significance in your life anymore, as you devote most of your time attending to the needs of a particular child. You need to make everyone understand that:

- Children with ADHD might exhibit behaviors that can disrupt everyone in the family.

- They are typically disorganized and can be easily distracted that they tend to keep other family members waiting, but they don't do it intentionally.

- They can hear instructions, but they don't have the ability to absorb what you want them to do, so don't expect them to obey.

- They start a task but forget to finish them, and leave everything behind without cleaning up.

- They might say things without thinking that might put you in an embarrassing spot.

- They sometimes demand attention in the most inappropriate time, and those with impulsivity issues often cut in conversations.

- Those who are hyperactive can practically tear the house apart, or do things that can bring physical harm upon themselves.

- They don't like to hit the sack even if they need to, and you might find that challenging and might even wear anyone's patience thin.

Understanding the condition can somehow help ease the situation. Expect everything to be difficult at first, and it might take a while before everything can go smoothly. Everything will be fine in the end if you will remain united on your goals.

ADHD and the Other Children in the Family

The behaviors of a child with ADHD make other children in the family deal with challenges like:

- Getting less attention as compared to their sibling with ADHD.

- They may be sharply reprimanded when they committed an error while their achievements might be taken for granted, or do not weigh that much.

- They may be blamed for their sibling's misbehavior under their supervision during the absence of their parents.

- They might find themselves jealous of their sibling with ADHD, and might even harbor resentment towards that sibling.

ADHD and the Parents

Parents are greatly affected if they have children who suffer from ADHD. They need to balance everything while giving full attention to their child with such condition. They need to have the ability to carefully plan things. They also need utmost patience not only for their child with ADHD, but also their other children who might begin to feel jealous about the attention given to their ADHD-afflicted sibling.

It is important for parents to keep their bodies in fit and healthy. They also need to be emotionally strong when dealing with the situation. The demands of a child suffering from ADHD can drain them physically and emotionally, and add to that is the concern for their other children.

The condition is frustrating for both parents and the child. Their patience will be tested especially during the time when the child with ADHD can only hear, but not listen. They can hear the commands, but cannot execute.

The whole thing can be stressful for the parents, but they know they should hold on through the end if they want to help their child and keep their family intact.

Sometimes, frustration can pave way to anger, and later guilt will set in for getting angry at the child who doesn't even want to be born that way, and who cannot make things the way they should.

If you have a child with ADHD, then you should be able to master how to combine consistency and compassion in order to help that child. Living in a home full of love and providing the right structure is the best thing that you can give your child who is trying to manage his or her condition.

Learn how to effectively parent a child with ADHD as the succeeding chapters give you helpful guide on how to go about it, and avoid possible trouble with your other children.

## Chapter 18: Consider A Yoga Or Tai Chi Class

Some small studies indicate that yoga may be helpful for people with ADHD. Research published in 2013 reported significant improvements in hyperactivity, anxiety, and social problems in boys with ADHD who practiced yoga regularly.

Some early studies suggest that tai chi also may help improve ADHD symptoms. Researchers found that teenagers with ADHD who practiced tai chi weren't as anxious or hyperactive. They also daydreamed less and displayed fewer inappropriate emotions when they participated in tai chi classes twice a week for five weeks.

What About Supplements?

Treatment with supplements may help improve symptoms of ADHD. These supplements include:

zinc

L-carnitine

vitamin B6

magnesium

However, results have been mixed. Herbs like ginkgo, ginseng, and passionflower also may help calm hyperactivity.

Supplementing without a doctor's oversight can be dangerous — particularly in children. Talk to your doctor if you're interested in trying these alternative therapies. They can order a blood test to measure current levels of a nutrient in your body before you start taking supplements.

Develop structure and neat habits—and keep them up

To organize a room, home, or office, categorize your objects, deciding which are necessary and which can be stored or discarded. To organize yourself, get in the habit of taking notes and writing lists. Maintain your newly organized structure with regular, daily routines.

**Create space.** Ask yourself what you need on a daily basis, and find storage bins or closets for things you don't. Designate specific areas for things like keys, bills, and other items that can be easily misplaced. Throw away things you don't need.

**Use a calendar app or day planner.** Effective use of a day planner or a calendar on your smartphone or computer can help you remember appointments and deadlines. With electronic calendars, you can also set up automatic reminders so scheduled events don't slip your mind.

**Use lists.** Make use of lists and notes to keep track of regularly scheduled tasks, projects, deadlines, and appointments. If you decide to use a daily planner, keep all lists and notes inside it. You also have many options for use on your smartphone or computer. Search for "to do" apps or task managers.

**Deal with it now.** You can avoid forgetfulness, clutter, and procrastination by filing papers, cleaning up messes, or returning phone calls immediately, not sometime in the future. If a task can be done in two minutes or less, do it on the spot, rather than putting it off for later.

Tame your ADD/ADHD paper trail

If you have adult ADD / ADHD, a major part of your disorganization might be with paperwork—in endless piles or strewn across your kitchen, desk, or office. Take an afternoon to set up a paperwork system that works for you.

**Set up a filing system.** Use dividers or separate file folders for different types of documents (such as medical records, receipts, and income statements). Label and color-code your files so that you can find what you need quickly.

**Deal with mail on a daily basis.** Set aside a few minutes each day to deal with the mail, preferably as soon as you bring it inside. It helps to have a designated spot where you can sort the mail and either trash it, file it, or act on it.

**Go paperless.** Minimize the amount of paper you have to deal with. Request electronic statements and bills instead of paper copies. You can also reduce junk mail by opting out of the Direct Marketing Association's (DMA) Mail Preference Service.

Time management tips for adult ADD/ADHD

Adults with attention deficit disorder often have a different perception of how time passes. To align your sense of time with everyone else, use the oldest trick in the book: a clock.

**Become a clock-watcher.** Use a wristwatch or highly visible wall or desk clock to help you keep track of time. When you start a task, make a note of the time by saying it out loud or writing it down.

**Use timers.** Allot yourself limited amounts of time for each task and use a timer or alarm to alert you when your time is up. For longer tasks, consider setting an alarm to go off at regular intervals to keep you productive and aware of how much time is going by.

**Give yourself more time than you think you need.** Adults with ADD/ADHD are notoriously bad at estimating how long it will take to do something. For every thirty minutes of time you think it will take you to get someplace or complete a task, give yourself a cushion by adding ten minutes.

**Plan to be early and set up reminders.** Write down appointments for fifteen minutes earlier than they really are. Set up reminders to ensure you leave on time and make sure you have everything you need ahead of time so you're not frantically looking for your keys or phone when it's time to go.

Prioritization tips for adult ADD/ADHD

Because adults with ADD/ADHD often struggle with impulse control and jump from one subject to another, completing tasks can be difficult and large projects can seem overwhelming. To overcome this:

**Decide what's first.** Ask yourself what is the most important task you need to accomplish, and then order your other tasks after that one.

**Take things one at a time.** Break down large projects or tasks into smaller, manageable steps.

**Stay on task.** Avoid getting sidetracked by sticking to your schedule, using a timer to enforce it if necessary

Learn to say no

Impulsiveness can lead adults with ADD/ADHD to agree to too many projects at work or make too many social engagements. But a jam-packed schedule can leave you feeling overwhelmed, overtired, and affect the quality of your work. Turning things down may improve your ability to accomplish tasks, keep social dates, and live a healthier lifestyle. Check your schedule first before committing to something new.

Get in the driver's seat to control your budget

An honest assessment of your financial situation is the first step to getting budgeting under control. Start by keeping track of every expense, no matter how small, for a month (yes, 30 days). This will allow you to effectively analyze where your money is going. You may be surprised how much you're spending on unnecessary items and impulse purchases. You can then use this snapshot of your spending habits to create a monthly budget based on your income and needs.

Figure out what you can do to avoid straying from your budget. For example, if you're spending too much at restaurants, you can make an eating-in plan and factor in time for grocery shopping and meal preparation.

## Chapter 19: Natural Adhd Treatments

Attention deficit hyperactivity disorder or ADHD is a common mental disorder, particularly in children. It affects 3 to 5 percent of all children, perhaps as many as 2 million children and can persist into adolescence and adulthood. The disease, once called hyper kinesis, is most often treated with drugs such as Ritalin; however, there is a strong movement to look for natural ADHD treatments.

The traditional drug treatments for ADHD consist of stimulants such as Ritalin or amphetamines such as Dexedrine or Adderall.These drugs, however, can produce side effects. The side effects can be psychological in nature, ranging from depression to psychotic symptoms or even hallucinations. Other side effects may be physical such as loss of appetite, insomnia, and stomachaches. These drugs also have the risk of addiction. Rather than taking these drugs, many parents and physicians are taking a more holistic approach to the problem, taking into consideration diet, lifestyle, and personality.

Natural ADHD treatments are used to gently and effectively treat the symptoms of ADHD while at the same time helping the child live a balanced life. The natural approach is less harmful and has a better chance of curing the problem altogether than traditional drugs. The key to natural ADHD treatments is finding the combination that works best for your child. Often this involves some trial and error at first. Once a natural treatment is found to work, however, the results can be amazing.

Diet

Diet is the first thing that should be examined when looking for natural ADHD cures. Often there is a particular food or combination of foods that is contributing to the ADHD symptoms. Start by eliminating or cutting down on the consumption of certain foods from the diet for a two-week period. These foods are dairy products, junk food, chocolate, processed meats, fried foods, food colorings, fruit juices and NutraSweet. This may seem extreme, however, after the initial period you may start introducing these foods back into the diet. Add one food every other day to see what, if anything, results. Keep a food and behavior diary during this test period so you can study the results.

On an ongoing basis, keep the diet high in whole foods emphasizing vegetables and whole grains. Eat a diet that is balanced in carbohydrates and proteins. Limit the amount of junk food, especially sugar. Drink juices that are diluted to decrease the intake of sugar.

Supplements

Vitamin and mineral supplements are often quite helpful as a natural ADHD treatment. There are certain vitamins that may be lacking in the body which are causing or adding to the ADHD. Vitamin C and Niacinamide together form a combination that may help ADHD patients. Niacinamide is a form of vitamin B3. These two vitamins may help reduce hyperactivity and restlessness and allow children to improve their concentration.

Colloidal minerals also called fully chelated minerals offer the best form of mineral supplement and are available through many health food stores. They can provide the missing minerals from the diet and can help to calm overactive minds.

Herbs

There are many herbs known to be helpful in the natural treatment of ADHD. They can reduce mood swings and increase alertness. The reduction of prescription drugs along with herbal treatments often helps the patient improve memory and concentration while not in a haze. Some of the more popular herbs for treating ADHD are Chamomile, Evening Primrose Oil, Fresh Lemon balm, and Gotu Kola, among others.

Medication

The most common and effective types of medication used as an ADHD treatment option are stimulants. It is unclear at this time why a stimulant (which speeds up brain activity) is having such positive effects on such symptoms as hyperactivity and impulsivity. However, around 75% of patients are having a successful treatment rate.

## WHAT TO AVOID EATING WHEN YOU HAVE ADHD

Officially, most medical researchers state that changing your diet will not affect your ADHD symptoms. Most of these researchers don't have ADHD. They may be right that diet changes don't affect the ADHD symptoms directly. However, evidence shows that changing your diet can help with factors that affect the severity of our ADHD symptoms.

One researcher has identified a direct link between diet and the severity of ADHD symptoms. Dr. Lidy Pelsser is a researcher at the ADHD Research Center in the Netherlands. She did a study on children with ADHD and their diets. Children were put on a strict diet then taken off of it. Dr.

Pelsser reported that parents and teachers saw a remarkable change in the severity of the children's ADHD symptoms.

NPR reported that Dr. Pelsser explains the relationship by saying, "The skin is affected, but a lot of people get eczema because of a latex allergy or because they are eating a pineapple or strawberries." Dr. Pelsser explains the outcome of the study by saying, "After the diet, they were just normal children with normal behavior," she says. No longer were they easily distracted or forgetful, and the temper tantrums subsided." (NPR, 2011, Study: Diet May Help ADHD Kids More Than Drugs)

Stay Away From Caffeine

If you have ADHD then there are many reasons to take caffeine out of your diet. Caffeine reacts with any ADHD medication that is stimulant based. Stimulant based ADHD medications include Adderall, Ridelin, etc. These medications work by stimulating your system. When you mix them with caffeine then the effects are "supercharged".

Caffeine also adds to anxiety. Caffeine causes a person to be jittery and anxious.Anxiety is one of the most common symptoms with ADHD. Caffeine can take ADHD's anxiety symptoms and cause them to be worse. Why would a person with anxiety want to take something that makes anxiety worse?

Eat Protein

Eating a diet rich in protein has multiple affects that help ADHD. This should include lean proteins such as fish, chicken, lean beef, and lean pork. ADHD symptoms are caused by some areas of the brain producing more chemicals then others. Protein helps our brains neurotransmitters to produce more chemicals. This helps alleviate the chemical deficit.

Our bodies also use protein to stabilize our blood sugar. Blood sugar lows can cause us to have headaches, become irritable, and cause trouble controlling our temper. High blood sugar levels can cause us to be anxious, have an excess energy, have trouble paying attention, etc. Both of these conditions mimic a lot of our ADHD symptoms. By keeping our blood sugar on an even keel then we help lessen our ADHD symptoms.

Eat Balanced Meals

Everything must be done in moderation. A balanced diet helps control blood sugar, body fat; all our body systems work better. Our diets should include vegetables, complex carbohydrates, fruits, and protein. Several parents of children with ADHD and adults with ADHD have seen their symptoms lessen with a balanced diet.

ADDitude magazine states, "Ned Hallowell, M.D., founder of the Hallowell Center for Cognitive and Emotional Health, in Sudbury, Massachusetts, and New York City, advises all of his ADHD patients to think about their plates when preparing a meal. Half of the plate, he recommends, should be filled with fruits or vegetables, one-fourth with a protein, and one-fourth with carbohydrates." (ADDitude magazine, 2013)

## Use Supplements for Deficiencies

Today, everyone is leading busy lives.Even our children go to school, after school events, plays, band recitals, etc. Adults have to balance ever increasing demands at work, time with their family, getting children to and from school functions, and still try to watch their diet. This makes it difficult to get all the necessary fruits and vegetables into our diets.

Supplements make it easy to get the required nutrients.A daily multi-vitamin provides 100% of the daily amounts of a variety of vitamins and minerals. This is a great place to start. Fish oil has also been found to help with ADHD symptoms. Look at your individual diet. What foods are you not eating enough of? Then find a multi-vitamin that will give you those nutrients.

## Eliminate Foods One at a Time

It can be easy to find out if a food is increasing your ADHD symptoms.Simply start by identifying foods that may be worsening your ADHD symptoms. Possible culprits can be caffeine or sugar as listed above. Others may be MSGs, yellow or red food coloring. Pick one thing such as caffeine then eliminate it from your diet for a couple of weeks. The first few days will be necessary to get it out of your system. If your ADHD symptoms get better then eliminate that food from your diet.You can repeat this process for sugar or other foods to see which ones help you.

Keep Educating Yourself

ADHD research has increased multiple times over in the last 20 to 30 years. Researchers are constantly learning more about our ADHD symptoms, their causes, and how to lessen their effects on our lives. Personal research helps you stay up to date on new advances. This is not as daunting a task as it sounds. There are many websites, blogs, and even a social network dedicated to ADHD.

## Chapter 20: Tips To Decrease Side Effects

Stomach upsets, weight loтт, inтomnia are all common тide

effects of ADHD medicationт. Often they are mild, not laтting beyond the firтt few weekт but not alwayт. For many kids, the battle with тide effects is constant.

ADHD medicationт are extremely beneficial for the vaтt majority

of kidт, but most will have one or more тide effectт,".

Whether you will then switch to a different medication will depend on the benefits and how significant the тide effectт are.

If the medication iт helping the ADHD symptoms, тometimeт it'т

worth it to tough it out and see if the тide effectт go away, which they often do. Other times you can work around the тide effectт, тuch aт giving the medication with food to avoid stomachaches. But sometimes the тide effectт prove

unacceptable and a change of medication iт required,".

24

Stomach and Appetite Troubleт

Stomach upтetт often diтappear within a few weekт, aт the

child'т тyтtem gets uтed to the ADHD medication. Many

children, however, continue to have appetite problems. Try

these three тimple steps:

☐ Give ADHD medication with food. If morning medication is taken after breakfaтt, there's less risk of тtomach upsets.

☐ Encourage healthy тnacking. Have lots of healthy after-

тchool and bedtime тnackт available. High-protein and energy bars, protein shakes, and liquid mealт тuch aт

Carnation Instant Breakfast and Ensure are good options.

☐ Change dinnertime. Eat later in the evening, when your child's medication has worn off.

Headaches

Headaches, like stomach upsets, are related to taking ADHD

medication without food in the stomach. "It's like having a strong cup of coffee on an empty stomach." Try these tips:

☐ Always give ADHD medication with food. Without food, ADHD medication gets absorbed more quickly, which causes blood levels of the medication to rise quickly.

This can trigger a headache.

☐ Consider long-acting medication. Headache can also be a rebound effect when medication is wearing off

25 quickly, and is more common with short-acting medications. It may be

neceттary to switch to a longer-acting verтion of the drug or try a different ADHD medication altogether.

Difficulty Sleeping

Sleep problemт are common for children with ADHD, partly

because of the child's naturally high activity level. For many kids, inтomnia occurт when a тtimulant medication wears off.

For otherт, the stimulant affects them much like coffee affectт

adults.

To offset тleep problemт, it helps to develop a bedtime ritual for the child. Thiт routine will help the child calm down at bedtime

and get the sleep they need. Try these tipт:

☐ Give the morning doтe of ADHD medication earlier in the day.

☐ Discuss medication changes with the doctor. It may be

neceттary   to   try   тhorter-acting medicationт.

☐  Don't  allow  your  child  to  drink caffeinated beverages.

Cocoa and many sodas, coffeeт, and teas all contain caffeine. A child who drinkт theтe in the afternoon or evening may be toттing and turning at bedtime.

☐ Ertabliт a тleep-only zone. Your child'т bedroom тhould be dedicated to тleep -- not for homework, not for entertainment. Move the computer, radio, television, toyт, and games to another room. A few 26 stuffed animalт are fine, but there should be no other distractions.

☐ Teach your child to relax at bedtime. A тpecial blanket or a stuffed animal can help a child fall aтleep. But it's beтt to avoid bedtime activities that depend on a parent'т preтence -- like rocking or holding the child until sleep comes.

☐  Ertabliт  consistency.  Bedtimeт  and waking timeт

should be the same seven days a week. Waking times

are more important than bedtimes in establishing sleep

rhythms. It is easier to enforce a waking time than a bedtime. "Sleeping in" can be a sign that the child is not getting enough sleep.

☐ Establish daytime routines. Regular meal and activity

times help, too. Routines make it easier for children to

"wind down" to sleep.

☐ Discourage midnight visits. Waking up at night can become a habit for children. It can also be a way to get attention. While you don't want to let a child cry

themselves to sleep, it's best to discourage middle-of-the-night visits with mom and dad or midnight snacks.

Also, don't allow interesting toys near the child's bed (a stuffed animal or two is fine).

☐ Avoid тleep medications. Мedicationт ттop working over time, and may affect daytime alertness. They may

alтo wear off during the night, and cauтe night waking.

Some medicationт may cauтe nightmareт or other typeт

of sleep problemт. If medicationт are abтolutely

necessary, talk to your child'т doctor about тafe and effective treatmentт.

27 ☐ Conтider medical problems. Allergieт, asthma, or conditionт that cause pain can disrupt тleep. If your child snores loudly and/or pauтeт in breathing, medical evaluation iт necessary. Conтult your phyтician for help

with the poттible medical cauтeт of sleep problemт.

Tics

Ticт are involuntary motor movementт тuch aт exceттive eye

blinking, throat clearing, тniffing, blinking, shrugging, or head-turning. About one in three boyт and one in тix girls with ADHD

will develop tics with or without medication. "ADHD

medications can bring out an underlying predisposition to ticт

but the medicationт don't cause tics," .

Chart your child's unusual movementт. Talk to your pediatrician if you think your child may have ticт. A change in medication, or combining medicationт, may help.

Growth Problemт

Some children taking тtimulant ADHD medications loтe their appetite, which in turn can affect weight and growth. Most children may have a tendency not to gain weight over the first тix to nine months of treatment, but then resume normal weight. Over two yearт, the majority of children weigh three to five poundт leтт than they would if not on medicationт --

and might be 0.1 to 0.5 incheт ттhorter than their peerт.

"A very ттmall group of children iт very тentitive to theтe

medicationт,". "They loтe their appetite, which means they lose 28

a тignificant amount of weight -- тo they don't grow." The ADHD

medication by itself doeт not stunt growth. Rather, the child doesn't eat enough to get necessary nutrition for growth. Try theтe tipт:

☐ Plot a growth chart. Make sure the pediatrician takeт

height and weight prior to starting ADHD drugs.

Meaтurementт тhould be made and charted three to four timeт a year.

☐ Encourage snacking. If your child has loтt weight, encourage тnacking on high-protein nutrition bars, protein тhakeт, and liquid mealт тuch aт Carnation Instant Breakfaтt and Ensure.

☐ Studies show that most kids will catch up in height and weight. "ADHD kids are often a couple of years behind other kids in growth maturation and puberty, so

parents tend to worry about them,". "Puberty will just come later, probably at 15 rather than 13. By puberty, almost all kids have caught up to the normal height and weight they would have had if they had not been taking the medications."

Noticeable Mood Changes

For many kids, ADHD medications bring a sunnier mood and more enjoyment in life. But occasionally, a child becomes too quiet and seems sadder, depressed, moody an extreme

emotional change. Such emotional changes could prove to be

an unacceptable side effect or perhaps a sign that the dose of medication is too high. If the moodiness is especially noticeable

29 when the medication is wearing off, it could be a sign of what's

137

known aт "rebound effect," and may require a change in ADHD

medication.

"The medication may be making the kid irritable, as happens more often with younger kids," тayт Parker. "But if the child iт

feeling тad, depressed, or extremely irritable and the mood doeтn't lift in a week or two that might not be тomething you can work around. The cure should never be worse than the disease, so it may be a тign to change the medication." Try thiт

tip:

☐ Chart your child's mood changes. Note your child'т

highт and lows, and the time of day they occur. Then talk to the pediatrician

Rebound of Difficult Behaviorт

Often the ADHD тymptomт are under control early in the day, when the blood haт a high level of medication. Aт the medicine

wearт off and leaveт the body, there may be a rebound effect.

The difficult behaviorт may return, often worse than before.

This iт not a true тide effect, but rather a reтult of medication wearing off. If your child has afternoon irritability and trouble

concentrating, it could be a sign of rebound effect. Try these tipт:

☐ Chart your child's behavior. Note the time of day that behaviors change, and what'т happening.

30 ☐ Talk to the doctor. If there тeemтto be a pattern of ADHD тymptomт appearing in the afternoon or evening, the child may need another short-acting medication in the afternoon. Or the child may need a different combination of medicationт, including a nonstimulant or low-doтe tricyclic antidepressant.

Dizzineтт

Dizzineтт can occur when the ADHD medication doтe is too high. If you notice your child getт dizzy, have your child drink fluids and get your child'т blood preттure checked right away. If that'т normal, try thiт tip:

☐ Talk to thedoctor. It may be time to тwitch to an extended-releaтe medication to тmooth out the highs and lowт in medication levels in the blood.

Nausea, Tiredness

With the nonттimulant drug Strattera, nauтea and excessive tiredness are common side effects in the first few weekт. To

help the child build up a tolerance to the medication, try theтe

tipт:

☐ Start with a low doтe. Increaтe the doтe by a тmall amount every one to two weekт.

☐ Change dosing. Give the doтe at night or divide the doтe

into morning and late afternoon доѕадет

31 In September 2005 the FDA iѕѕued a public health adviѕory

about rare reportѕ of ѕuicidal thinking in children and adolescents taking Strattera. Strattera haѕ been aѕѕociated with an increaѕed riѕk of ѕuicidal thinking in children and adoleѕcentѕ

with ADHD. Youth who start thiѕ drug require cloѕe monitoring for suicidal thinking or unuѕual changeѕ in behavior for the first few months or after the doѕage iѕ changed.

Increased Heart Rate & Pulse

These ѕide effects develop when a child takeѕ an ADHD drug pluѕ a decongeѕtant like Sudafed. "You're mixing two potent stimulants together,". "That'ѕ when we get a call that a kid is getting panicky at school only to find out the parents gave him cold medicine that morning." In fact, pѕeudoephedrine

(Sudafed) dramatically increases all ᴛide effectᴛ from ᴛtimulantᴛ.

Try theᴛe tipᴛ:

☐ Uᴛe a naᴛal ᴛpray when your child has a cold.

☐ Skip the ADHD medication when your child iᴛ ᴛtuffed up

and needᴛ a decongeᴛtant.

☐ Or, chooᴛe a cold medicine that doeᴛn't contain pseudoephedrine.

## Chapter 21: Energy-Based Activities

Children with ADHD are high in energy. They are often asked to sit still at school for long periods. Outlets for energy must be taken into account when planning their daily/weekly schedule. Many parents often expect children to complete homework and chores immediately upon arriving home to prevent the battle later to get them re-focused. For ADHD children, this can often compound the problems they have already had all day.

It is essential for all children with ADHD to "decompress" when they get home. Having time to burn up energy or to just "zone out" and defocus can help them let out all the hyperactivity they have been holding in all day. This can be done through structured or unstructured physical activity that the child enjoys. The choice of activity would typically be the child's.

Chores that involve action are going to be better suited to children with ADHD than ones done standing still. A child with ADHD will struggle to stand and hand wash dishes but may do much better push mowing the lawn. They will do better with chores that are less tedious and require less attention to detail.

Structured energy outlets are also important. These can be something as simple as bike riding, playing active games, or other family activities that involve movement and structure. When possible, having a sport or activity can help the child. Tae Kwon Do is one that provides movement, structure, discipline, and focus. The child is learning several skills at one time, burning energy, and having fun. Dance, sports, and other movement-based activities can all fulfill this role. Regardless, the child needs to enjoy the activity.

School-Based Activities

Children with ADHD struggle with school. They are expected to stay still and focused for more extended periods then they are typically capable of. They are expected to do the multi-step process. For example, get out your paper and pencil, do your assignment, and then turn it in. They also have the added level of peer pressure because if they are labeled the "bad kid" that no one wants to be friends with them.

Many schools in the past have pushed parents to medicate and are not always receptive to alternative ways of handling behaviors. However, over time, this policy is changing. Schools are becoming more open to school and parent-based collaborations and open to a child not being medicated. It is important to consider an IEP or 504 plan when needed to ensure that accommodations are known to everyone, clear and understandable, and followed.

Parent-School Cooperation

Parents need to maintain regular contact with school personal on both behaviors and possible interventions to use. Parents working with teachers need to develop a system of tracking school assignments, much like chores. This can include emails or text messages, written notes, or an agenda. When possible, the child should be responsible for writing the assignment. But having a backup system is important until the child routinely knows their homework assignments and brings them home. Parents can ask the school to provide a set of books to be kept at home, allowing homework to be completed if and when the child does not remember to bring the needed books home.

Parents need to make sure the routine they develop has time for school work. The amount of time will vary based on the child's grade, focus, and abilities. For children with many assignments, breaking up the homework time will work better than trying to have the child sit and do it all at once. Using the Premack principle and having children do the subject they like least first also helps.

In the classroom, the teacher needs to use some of the same strategies discussed with the parenting interventions. Tasks and assignments need to be broken down into smaller parts. The teacher needs to have the child repeat back directions for tests, assignments, and homework to make sure he/she understood them. Having written instructions help with re-directing the child if he/she is off task, much like re-directing back to the chore chart. Parents and school personal through communication can attempt to adapt what works in one setting to the other setting to help with consistency

Intervention Strategies

Children are often asked to sit and stay focused for long periods at school. This scenario is precisely what children with ADHD struggle with. The school must be able to identify ways for the children to release their pent up energy that is acceptable in the classroom. The purpose of recess is to give all children breaks during the day. For children with ADHD, this can be even more important. Parents and teachers will have to work together to map out the best school day for the child.

Taking more frequent breaks is a typical school modification. The child is allowed to leave the room, use the restroom, get a drink, or quietly sit in another area of the room at specific times. The breaks are planned and specific. The child is told the times/reason they can take the break and where. Another adult, like an aide, is assigned to the child as needed during this time for supervision. The child is not allowed to just randomly go where he/she wants or when he/she wants.

Some children do best if they can keep their bodies physically engaged as much as possible. Modifications to sitting arrangements is one such example. A large rubber band stretched around the front chair legs can give a child with ADHD something to quietly bounce his legs against. Another option is chairs that incorporate yoga balls into them iso the child has to engage his/her core to keep balanced. However, any activities like these need to well thought out. Fidget spinners have become such a nuisance in some schools that they have been banned. Whatever the child is going to be directed to do cannot become a distraction to the child or the other students.

Academic performance is one of the best predictors of success for children with ADHD as adults. Parents and teachers can work together and with the child to help them improve their academic performance. Through the school, the child can be taught more effective study skills to help them study better. Interventions can be used to help the students stay focused and on task. Many times poor grade performance is more a result of lack of attention rather than a lack of ability.

Students with ADHD struggle to stay on task and focused. The teacher and parent can work together to identify how to reduce and eliminate distractions in the classroom. For example, having very few things on the child's desk, having the child sit where they cannot easily look out a window can help. Sitting in the front row or close to the teacher can also help ensure the child has less distractions. The teacher is also better able to recognize when they are distracted and assist them. These ideas can also be incorporated at home where the child does their homework.

It is important also to help the child stay focused while studying. The teacher can help keep the student engaged through calling on them and giving them feedback frequently. The teacher and student can develop a prearranged signal that the teacher uses to draw the student's attention back to their assignment. The child can also be presented with a daily "report card" much like the one discussed that parents could use. The report card can have some positive behaviors and score how well the child engaged in these behaviors. These interventions must be done in a way that the child is not singled out form peer and made to feel awkward in the class and/or that peers begin to shun the child.

Testing

Test-taking can be very anxiety-provoking for children with ADHD. Research shows they often do not score as high as they can accomplish on standardized testing. This can be true in the classroom. Teaching effective test-taking either through the school or at home, can help decrease this. Helping the child learn to review the material regularly, reading directions twice, and re-checking work can all help a child improve their test scores. Again role-playing and modeling are more effective in teaching than just telling.

Testing away from distractions, having someone read the directions, and extending or eliminating time limits can help children with ADHD test better.

Skill Building

The school can also provide organizational support. A teacher or an aide can help the child with monitoring and helping organize lockers, agendas, and backpacks. A note-taking partner or access to the teacher's notes can assist the student in learning to take better notes. It also fills in the gaps until the student is taking better notes. Reminders to turn in completed homework. All of these strategies can assist the child both ensure homework is completed and turned in and provides modeling and practice until the child can successfully master these skills.

Educational Plan

Some schools will work with parents informally to devise teaching and education strategies that work for the child. However, at times, it is important to have a formalized written educational plan that spells out the exact modification for the child. The program can discuss education adjustments, such being given shorter assignments or longer test-taking time. Behavioral interventions, such as more frequent breaks, also need to be included in the plan.

Parents can request these plans for their children through the school or local Area Education Area. The process can be very time-consuming and drag out. Many parents get frustrated with the process. But, in the long run, it can be very beneficial to the child. The two choices are a 504 plan or an IEP (Individualized Educational Plan).

These are unique plans that both focus on helping the student receive the best quality of education in the "least restrictive" environment. However, they have different qualifications and service focus. An IEP is for a student with an identified diagnosed disability (ADHD qualifies) that can be documented to be negatively impacting their education based on Department of Educational criteria. It is important to note that a child can have a disability and not qualify for an IEP.

The student must have a disability that affects a primary life function to qualify for a 504 plan. The primary life function does not have to be educational. The 504 plan is a better option for a student that can function well in a regular educational environment but needs some accommodations, such as longer testing time. The 504 is typically less restrictive and less stigmatizing. It is often the better fit for a child with ADHD unless they have other school-based problems or learning disabilities.

Summary

Children with ADHD need to learn how to control and manage their behaviors, develop and maintain peer relationships, and learn skill-building. These behaviors are not developed solely through the use of medication. There must be a strong team (including parents, school personnel, and the child) who develop behavioral interventions that do not just correct the child but helps him/her learn how to adapt and cope.

Research shows that children with a strong positive parenting bond, good sibling/peer relationships, and academic success have the best long-term outcomes as adults. When choosing interventions with these goals in mind, children with ADHD can thrive. This book outlines several different methods and interventions for parents to use. Parents have to choose the ones that work best for their child, family, and lifestyle.

Interventions that focus on a variety of aspects can help develop a comprehensive, complete program that allows the parent to assist their child. The idea is to make sure the child with ADHD has the correct tools so that over time, they can take over managing their own lives and behaviors. The child can use these strategies into adulthood.

Parents need to consider getting outside support if they feel overwhelmed and/or none of the strategies suggested appear to be working. Outside help can come in many forms, such as parenting support groups, in-home skill-building services, school support, and mental health professionals.  Parents need to choose the support that helps them.

## Chapter 22: 8 Proven Methods Of Managing Adhd

Many adults who have ADHD feel overwhelmed at times with regular life chores and responsibilities as they are unable to manage time and errands effectively. This article deals with workable, practical and useful ways that can be incorporated into daily life scheduling in order to bring about an organized, structured and more productive lifestyle for ADHD-ers.

Being diagnosed with ADHD can be overwhelming for many people who can find it difficult to even attend to routine chores as even these look like obstacles to them; thus, understanding the basics of proper time management is important for them to stay atop things. This includes daily planning done effectively on a regular basis to control stress levels and actually get work done right on time, every time, minimizing hassles all round for ADHD-ers.

Sometimes, the day may pass by in a haze for ADHD-ers who may have sleepless nights considering they didn't get anything worthy accomplished and simply focusing on their long to- do list that calls for more enthusiasm than they can muster; this may leave them tired, disorganized, lacking creativity, contentment and energy.

These Eight Essential Tips are designed at helping ADHD-ers realize and focus on various abilities they can concentrate on in order to improve their lifestyles: take a look!

1. Easing the Pace: is very important for people with ADHD as being hyper-active and having a hurried pace only works to wear down limited stores of energy and enthusiasm to start and stick to tasks; thus, slowing down to a comfortable and realistic pace is very important to effectively handle jobs.

2. Setting Aside some 'Me-time': is another important ability ADHD-ers need to practice in order to give themselves the

importance they are due because their innate tendency to focus on other people's needs may at times deprive them of essential personal time and energy.

3. Learning more about Your own ADHD condition: is of utmost important in knowing how to handle it right as this disorder can manifest itself differently for different individuals.

4. Learn to categorize individual methods of learning and processing information that work best results for you as an ADHD-er and recognize ones that hinder your concentration abilities or feelings to interfere with enhancing right personal and professional decisions and actions in order to simplify your life.

5. Focus on your strong points and emphasize your key areas of expertise to always stay on top of the world as holding positive thoughts helps realize these into actions with fervent spirit and right efforts, ADHDing to a sense of accomplishment and raising self-esteem.

6. Be an optimist: as thinking along negative lines only brings down energy, enthusiasm and positive thoughts that can make a success of a task besides holding you down. Charge ahead with positive thinking!

7. Make Time for Time Planning: as daily planning at a fixed time for all tasks, big or small, is essential to the well-being of all ADHD-ers who may have difficulty attending to multiple chores, so may need to develop tools and strategies for proper time management and administration in order to ensure good beginnings result in happy and successful endings, including meeting goals.

8. Develop the ability to meet challenges head-on: attempt at stepping out of a comfort zone in order to bring novelty, creativity and higher degrees of motivation towards enhancing the quality of life, whether it means asking for a raise, taking up a new hobby, learning a new skill or finally pursuing a dream.

6 Tips For Slowing Down The ADHD Brain

If you are an adult suffering with ADHD, then you might recognize that although it is easy to say, slowing down can be a very difficult if not impossible thing to do at first glance.

No matter who you are there are numerous things that have to be done and all too often little time available to get them done. So then your mind starts to work at high speed in an attempt to achieve as much as it can and more. The result can be stress at not being able to meet your requirements, leading to you getting upset about the fact that it looks impossible. Because of this you use up lots of time worrying, and unfortunately little time enjoying yourself.

Whilst slowing down can be a complex thing to achieve it can be done. Here are six established methods to assist you to slow your brain ADHD or otherwise:

1. Put down your work

Set business hours and no matter what is left at the end of the day, walk away. Stand by your rules. Even though it is going to seem necessary to work overtime, avoid it at all cost. You will work better and more efficiently during the shorter hours of the day knowing that you must leave at a set time. And take weekends (or at least a couple of days a week off).

## 2. Commit to a regular obligation

Commit to a reason to get out of your house or out of your office each week. You may want to attend a class, possibly something that you have always wanted to do. Make sure that you 'pay' in advance for the class so that you have a reason to attend.

## 3. Arrange for a break with others

Few things are as enjoyable as having a night out with friends. This may be with colleagues, with friends, with family, or with members of another group.

## 4. Keep a diary

Writing in a diary requires that you stop, think about what you want to say, and then act on what you think. It helps you to deal with nervous tension and achieve clearness. make a resolution to write every day - even if only for a few minutes!

5. Switch your computer off two hours before bed

Because computers are an access point to interesting things, for ADHDers you can find yourself sitting at a computer until the early hours of the morning completely oblivious to what is happening around you. To make sure that this doesn't happen to you switch the computer off at least 2 hours before you plan to go to sleep so as to suitably relax and slow down at night.

6. Meditate

There are diverse methods of meditation, so find one that suits you, but you may want to consider mindfulness meditation. This is the action of keeping your mind in the present - whether you are walking, working or washing dishes. Make an effort to keep your mind in the here and now not the past or future.

It is fine to start doing this little by little, with short sessions spent in mindful meditation daily (possibly only 5 minutes at a time), after that building your performance as you become more at ease.

Planning Daily Life For Adults With ADHD

Those adults who have been diagnosed with ADHD or Attention Deficit Disorder as this neurological imbalance is known as in medical circles, will appreciate that attention to details is something they have often felt the lack of; this is not a conscious decision on their part but rather a result of the disorder, even for those who have objectives chalked out mentally and are eagerly waiting to achieve them. However, the sense of wishing themselves out of the efforts required to do the job right is common to all adults with ADHD and sometimes this attitude can be overwhelming when they need to focus on starting on any project. Therefore, a few practical tips on time management and workable approaches for enthusiastic beginnings and sticking to the job are more important than simply visualizing the end goal being met, which is what we tackle here.

That adults with ADHD find it difficult to begin right is very true in daily living as well as handling careers; this is why it is crucial for them to prioritize right beginnings to ensure happy endings and fruitful ones at that, especially to minimize stress and guilt factors that can lower productivity even with the best intentions when they started out. Here is where a daily planner would help adults with ADHD make planning a habit that supports structured and organized thought and action.

Quick tips for developing a daily routine for adults with ADHD include setting aside a time to plan, going over the list of tasks and the calendar. While the first helps to get a routine in order be it first thing in the morning or before hitting the sack at night when ADHD-ers are at their attentive best, the second helps to review the to-do list, which is essential for organized output and meeting objectives besides acting as a regular reminder for chores that need to be attended to. Then, routinely rewriting ely re-write this list to tick off those already attended to (gives a sense of achievement which helps build up enthusiasm for tackling new tasks) and note down new ones. The most important tasks should ideally head the list and bigger ones can be broken down to multiple steps to make them easy to tackle. Reviewing a calendar is the final step towards organized planning that helps adults with ADHD keep up to date with a checklist guiding them for right actions for this day and the next, blocking off appointments on a planner and ensuring commuting time is included in this so the remainder of the day can be planned for other tasks. Just a quarter of an hour kept aside to plan a schedule can thus help adults with ADHD tackle everyday situations with ease and lead a hassle-free life.

## Chapter 23: Choosing The Best Adhd Medication For Your Child

NIMH, the national institution in the United States that oversees mental health issues, conducted a thorough evaluation of different treatments for ADHD to help families of kids with ADHD choose the best treatment. Referred to as the MTA, the multimodal study involving children with ADHD demonstrated the effectiveness of a common stimulant medication called methylphenidate in treating the condition's symptoms, both on its own or when used with behavior modification. The same study discovered that treating the symptoms of ADHD in children with medication becomes more effective when the treatment is personalized and closely watched.

The MTA study also revealed these findings:

1. Medication not only plays an important role in treating the symptoms of ADHD in

children, but in adolescents and adults as well.

2. Medication has an enormous impact on young people who have ADHD, particularly by way of improving their attention, reducing their hyperactivity, and increasing their ability for smooth social interactions.

3. When kids with ADHD who also suffered from depression, anxiety, and other mental health conditions were given medication as part of both individual treatment and family treatment, better results were observed.

Things to Keep in Mind in Using ADHD Medication

1. Take as prescribed: Although medication is extremely effective in treating ADHD symptoms, it does work only when your child takes it as prescribed. ADHD medications are not like antibiotics, for example, that your child takes for a short period for infection treatment. ADHD medications are intended for addressing the symptoms of

ADHD and not the condition itself. The good news is that most kids with ADHD can achieve great results when they receive medication along with behavioral therapy.

2. Choices to make: There are two types of medications for treating the symptoms of ADHD, specifically the stimulant type and the non-stimulant type. Methylphenidate, amphetamines, and other stimulant medications have been proven to produce dramatic results after decades of use. On the other hand, the sole non-stimulant ADHD medication approved by the FDA atomoxetine is considered an effective alternative for kids with ADHD who did not achieve the expected results from stimulant medications or had other co-existing health issues.

3. Considering the side effects: It takes time before you will arrive at the best medication treatment for your child, especially since doctors usually have to consider different medications to determine which delivers the best results.

There is also the issue of side effects of some ADHD medications, in which case they will not be suitable for your child (side effects can be expected from both stimulant medications and non-stimulant medications).

The side effects that a child may experience after taking his medication can be controlled by adjusting the dosage, varying the time of administering the medication, or making the switch to another medication.

4. It takes two: There are two forms of stimulant ADHD medications, namely the long-acting and the short-acting forms. Long-acting stimulants, with their effects lasting between seven to twelve hours, are generally takes once daily. Meanwhile, the effects of a dose of short-acting stimulants usually last from four to five hours, which is why they are to be taken 2 to 3 times daily. Doctors may sometimes prescribe a mixture of the two forms of stimulant medications, although no studies have been made on the approach of using long-

acting stimulant medication with short-acting medication.

5. Easy does it: Kids who have trouble swallowing medication in the form of pills can receive their ADHD medication treatment in the form of chewable pills, liquid medicines, powders from opened capsules that are then sprinkled on food, and skin patches. Your child's doctor may start him on his stimulant medication at low doses, after which the dose will be increased every one to three weeks until your child's symptoms of ADHD are reduced.

Keep in mind that determining the proper dosage of stimulant medication can take a few months. As for non-stimulant ADHD medications, it is recommended that your child take them daily either once as a single dose or twice as half-doses. A large number of doctors will start a child with ADHD at a lower dose, after which he will gradually raise the dosage as the child adjusts to the non-stimulant. Building up to the proper dosage can take a few weeks, and full effects of the medication can be seen after a few more weeks.

6. Steer clear of hindrances: It is possible for the benefits of your kid's ADHD medications to be hindered by number of OTC medications. One example is diphenhydramine, which can cause some children with ADHD to experience agitation. This is the reason it is crucial that you inform your child's doctor of any prescription and OTC medications as well as vitamins and herbal supplements your child is taking.

7. Symptoms away means medication is okay: You will know that your child's ADHD medication is working when many of his symptoms are reduced or under control. Some of his symptoms may linger, however, but these can easily be treated with the help of behavior modification.

Know that it does take some time before your doctor can figure out the most effective dosage to give to your child that will produce the most desirable outcome. The fact is, up to ninety percent of kids with ADHD will hit upon more than one medication or even a mixture of different medications that will best reduce their symptoms.

8. Dealing with side effects: For most kids with ADHD receiving treatment with stimulant medication, some common side effects are expected, among which are problem sleeping, headaches, irritability, reduced appetite, stomach pain, and weight loss. After a few months of medication, these side effects usually subside. Meanwhile, reduced appetite, drowsiness, weight loss, mild irritability, and nausea are the common side effects of taking atomoxetine (non-stimulant), which normally get better after the patient's 1$^{st}$ month of treatment.

ADHD medication side effects may not usually be dangerous, but it is important that you inform your child's doctor about all of them, particularly when these side effects are causing discomfort or are keeping your child from going about his daily activities.

Each child with ADHD has a different response to medication. While some kids might show dramatic improvements, others may experience little relief (or none at all) from their symptoms. The side effects experienced by each child also differ, with some kids experiencing more side effects than the benefits expected from the medication taken. It does take time to find the proper medication as well as the correct dose because every child with ADHD has a different response.

It is important to always keep a close watch over your kid's medication. This is because ADHD treatment with medication goes beyond simply popping a pill and that is it. Instead, it involves monitoring the medication's side effects, keeping tabs on your child's reaction or feeling, and making adjustments to his medication's dosage. Failure to carefully monitor your child's medication can mean a more risky and less effective treatment.

Rest assured that placing your child on ADHD medication does not necessarily mean he needs to be on it for the rest of his life. With the consent of your child's doctor, you can make the decision of not giving any more ADHD medication to your child if he does not seem to be responding well. Just make sure to work with your child's doctor in gradually weaning him off the medication.

9. Call your child's doctor right away if he experiences the following rare side effects of his ADHD medication:

Becoming agitated

Complaining of rapid, skipped, or other forms of unusual heartbeats

Appearing to be depressed

Feeling dizzy or faint

Having shortness of breath or chest pains

Having hallucinations

Voicing suicidal thoughts

Having flu-like symptoms with no apparent cause

Itching

Passing dark urine

Feeling pain in the right upper belly

Having yellow skin/eyes

10. Fortunately, there are steps you could take should your child experience side effects after taking his ADHD medication:

Drowsiness – If your child feels sleepy during the day when taking his non-stimulant medication, you can (with your child's doctor's recommendation) switching the time of administration from morning to bedtime. You can also try halving his dosage and having him take his medication twice daily or decreasing the dosage to decrease his drowsiness.

Problem sleeping - Whatever is causing your child to sleep poorly or inadequately, it is important that you set up a healthy routine to help him get to sleep at bedtime. His bedtime routine can include brushing his teeth, taking a bath, or reading in bed. The key is to make sure these activities will enable him to wind down and fall asleep easier. In case your child still finds it difficult to sleep after following his bedtime routine, ask his doctor about giving the medication at an earlier time during the day.

Reduced appetite – To address this particular side effect of ADHD medication, consider having your child eat a big dinner when his medication starts wearing off, giving your child his dose after he has eaten his breakfast to make him hungry for his morning meal, and making sure there is food to be had when your child experiences hunger. It is also important to make sure your child is eating a balanced diet, coupled with appropriate high-caloric foods and beverages, to compensate for any weight loss. In case your child continues having a decreased appetite for a long time, ask his doctor about reducing the dose or stopping the medication altogether on the weekends or during the summer.

Rebound behavior – Some kids with ADHD who are taking stimulant medications can appear to be more irritable, with their symptoms of ADHD increasing later in the day. Referred to as rebounding by some doctors, it is possibly the result of the ADHD medication wearing off. Your child's doctor may suggest solving this problem by either going for a more long-lasting medication or having your child receive an immediate-release stimulant at a small dose late in the afternoon or early in the evening.

## Chapter 24: Medication For Adhd - The Positive And Negative Sides Of The Use Of Tenex To Treat Adhd

Tenex used for ADHD is a relatively recent innovation in the search for acceptable methods of treatment for children with ADHD. Although it offers an alternative to using the standard stimulant based medications, such as prescription medications, it is not without drawbacks and should be carefully considered before you decide to go that way with your child. A more common medicine for ADHD is Adderall. Adderall, Ritalin, and Concerta, are the most common medicines.

Tenex belongs to a group of medicines called antihypertensive drugs commonly used to control high blood pressure. Because it works become more closely associated by regulating the level of noradrenaline in the system Tenex and ADHD. By reducing this neurotransmitter may help alleviate Tenex stir and impulse control, making it attractive Creates improve ADHD.

The problem in the sight of drugs such as Tenex used for the treatment of ADHD is that it has had only limited success in alleviating the lack of concentration, hyperactivity, distractibility and impulsiveness associated with the condition. While appear to reduce some symptoms, others are not affected at all, so the success rate at best limited.

The reason that doctors and parents have been anxious to link Tenex and ADHD is that it can offer an alternative to using medications that can carry dangerous side effects. This is not to say that Tenex is without side effects. As with most medicines, there is always the danger of allergic reactions, and because Tenex acts specifically to lower blood pressure can also be a sedative effect, so that, in principle, a child in a stupor.

Tenex used for ADHD can also cause complications if your child requires medication for other conditions such as allergies or asthma, so there could be serious problems with this drug interaction. In short, as with any medical treatment, Tenex should never be seen as a cure all and you have to use to approach it with caution.

While continue to be linked Tenex and ADHD and is likely to be the subject of discussion for some time, there are other treatment methods concerned parents can turn to that does not carry the risk of side effects. Among these are changes in the diet, behavioral training and use of homeopathic treatments. Often reduce caffeine and sugar intake and remove wheat from the diet and the use of targeted education and behavioral techniques such as neurofeedback offer positive results without the use of medication altogether.

If your child requires some medical attention, the world of homeopathic treatment offers a much more effective alternative to Tenex used for ADHD. Products made from a special blend of herbs and herbal ingredients can work to address the chemical imbalances which cause ADHD, providing long-term results that not only convenience, but actually knew distressing symptoms.

ADHD is a difficult condition to treat, and frustrated parents desperately seeking all possible means for their children to live a normal, happy life. For this reason, drugs such as Tenex have emerged as possible solutions, but they should never be accepted at face value. Always stay informed and do not be afraid to explore all your options. Together, you and your doctor to find the right approach for your child.

## Chapter 25: Adhd Treatment Options

Receiving an official diagnosis of ADHD is the first concern of all parents and adult sufferers. Once it has been determined that this disorder is at work, there are two primary methods of treatment available:

Medication

Behavior Modification/Behavioral Therapy

Treatment is not the same for every ADHD sufferer. Some may take prescription medication to control symptoms, while others may decide they do not want to risk the side effects that may come with medication. Many will combine medication with therapy to modify their behaviors, others will only go through therapy and shun medicine completely.

You have to work closely with the medical professional that gave the diagnosis to determine the most suitable treatment for your condition or your child's condition. If you have concerns about medication, then bring those concerns to your therapist or doctor. They will be able to discuss all potential side effects and help you determine what is best for the patient sitting before them.

What Is Behavior Modification/Therapy?

Behavior modification is a fancy term for learning new skills and techniques for managing your ADHD symptoms. Most sufferers have trouble in school, work, and social situations because they have racing thoughts, cannot sit still, or cannot focus on one thing long enough to have a conversation or take instructions. They may also struggle with organizational skills, or may find that prioritizing their life and work is very difficult.

All of these problems can be overcome, or at least lessened, with behavioral modification. A therapist works with the ADHD sufferer to identify all behavioral problems associated with the disorder and develop new skills and behaviors that will make them more successful in daily life.

You can learn more about behavior modification and therapy as a treatment for ADHD in chapters eight and nine.

Do You Need Medication?

Some people require medication to control the symptoms of their ADHD, but others may get by without taking it or only taking it at certain times. There are clear benefits to prescription medication, since there is no cure for this disorder. Yet, there are also some risks and side effects that come with the medications most commonly prescribed for ADHD.

Before you make a decision on medication, talk with a medical professional you trust. Get their honest opinion on whether you can improve your symptoms through therapy alone, or whether you may need the help of medication. Most sufferers end up with a combination of medication and therapy.

## Chapter 26: What To Avoid Eating When You Have Adhd

Officially, most medical researchers state that changing your diet will not affect your ADHD symptoms. Most of these researchers don't have ADHD. They may be right that diet changes don't affect the ADHD symptoms directly. However, evidence shows that changing diet can help with factors that affect the severity of ADHD symptoms.

Stay Away From Caffeine

If you have ADHD then there are many reasons to take caffeine out of your diet. Caffeine reacts with any ADHD medication that is stimulant based. Stimulant based ADHD medications include Adderall, Ridelin, etc. These medications work by stimulating your system. When you mix them with caffeine then the effects are "supercharged". Caffeine also adds to anxiety. Caffeine causes a person to be jittery and anxious. Anxiety is one of the most common symptoms with ADHD.

Caffeine can take ADHD's anxiety symptoms and cause them to be worse. Why would a person with anxiety want to take something that makes anxiety worse?

## Eat Protein

Eating a diet rich in protein has multiple effects that help ADHD. This should include lean proteins such as fish, chicken, lean beef, and lean pork. ADHD symptoms are caused by some areas of the brain producing more chemicals then others. Protein helps our brains neurotransmitters to produce more chemicals. This helps alleviate the chemical deficit. Our bodies also use protein to stabilize our blood sugar. Blood sugar lows can cause us to have headaches, become irritable, and cause trouble controlling our temper. High blood sugar levels can cause us to be anxious, have an excess energy, have trouble paying attention, etc. Both of these conditions mimic a lot of our ADHD symptoms. By keeping our blood sugar on an even keel then we help lessen our ADHD symptoms.

## Eat Balanced Meals

Everything must be done in moderation. A balanced diet helps control blood sugar, body fat; all our body systems work better. Our diets should include vegetables, complex carbohydrates, fruits, and protein. Several parents of children with ADHD and adults with ADHD have seen their symptoms lessen with a balanced diet.

## Use Supplements for Deficiencies

Today, everyone is leading busy lives. Even our children go to school, after school events, plays, band recitals, etc. Adults have to balance ever increasing demands at work, time with their family, getting children to and from school functions, and still try to watch their diet. This makes it difficult to get all the necessary fruits and vegetables into your diets.

Supplements make it easy to get the required nutrients. A daily multi-vitamin provides 100% of the daily amounts of a variety of vitamins and minerals. This is a great place to start. Fish oil has also been found to help with ADHD symptoms. Look at your individual diet. What foods are you not eating enough of? Then find a multi-vitamin that will give you those nutrients.

Eliminate Foods One at a Time

It can be easy to find out if a food is increasing your child's ADHD symptoms. Simply start by identifying foods that may be worsening the ADHD symptoms. Possible culprits can be caffeine or sugar as listed above. Others may be MSGs, yellow or red food coloring. Pick one thing such as caffeine then eliminate it from diet for a couple of weeks. The first few days will be necessary to get it out of your system. If ADHD symptoms get better then eliminate that food from the diet. You can repeat this process for sugar or other foods to see which ones help most.

10 NUTRITIONAL AND LIFESTYLE RECOMMENDATIONS THAT CAN REDUCE THE SYMPTOMS OF ADHD

The classical core symptoms of ADHD can be tamed through nutritional and lifestyle adjustments. There are several actions that can be taken which will have a significant effect on the symptoms of ADHD.

Here are 10 nutritional and lifestyle recommendations that can reduce the symptoms of ADHD if adhered to.

Make sure you never get too hungry. The brain uses 20 percent of the body's total energy, which is more than any other human organ. Therefore, the brain relies on a regular supply of food for energy. Without the nutrition that food supplies, brain function will be negatively impacted. This will affect self-control, concentration, sleep, mood, motor skills and memory. By making sure you never get overly hungry and have a healthy snack always at hand, you will ensure your self-control and attention span are under your control. In situations that might test your patience, I recommend you plan ahead and ensure that you have eaten well beforehand.

Increase dopamine release. In the brain, dopamine functions as a neurotransmitter (a chemical released by neurons, a type of brain cell) which is connected to feelings of pleasure, satisfaction and reward. Dopamine also sharpens the mind and makes one more alert. Low dopamine levels have been found in people suffering from ADHD which may lead to difficulty in focusing attention. Tyrosine is an amino acid that encourages the brain to release dopamine. Tyrosine is found in high amounts in almonds, avocados, bananas, lima (butter) beans, pumpkin seeds and sesame seeds. By consuming these foods regularly, you will ensure your body has sufficient tyrosine to support dopamine release.

Increase serotonin release. It has been found that increasing dopamine release is not enough to control the symptoms of ADHD and serotonin levels were also of major importance. In fact, a balanced relationship between dopamine and serotonin was key to helping reduce ADHD symptoms. Serotonin is a neurotransmitter related to impulse control and aggression. Tryptophan is an amino acid the body uses to manufacture serotonin. Tryptophan is found in spirulina, spinach, watercress, soybeans, mushrooms, turnip greens, mustard greens, asparagus, broccoli, sunflower seeds and kidney beans. By consuming these foods regularly, you will ensure your body has sufficient tryptophan to support serotonin production.

Increase complex whole grain carbohydrate rich foods in your diet. Tryptophan is the least abundant amino acid and therefore, in a protein rich meal, tryptophan is the last amino acid to cross the blood brain barrier. It has to wait its turn after the other amino acids. On the other hand, evidence suggests that eating a complex carbohydrate meal with little but sufficient protein will increase the tryptophan available to the brain. The reason for this is when carbohydrate rich foods are consumed, the body releases insulin, which diverts other amino acids to the muscles but leaves tryptophan untouched. This provides a better ground for tryptophan to enter the brain and promote its calming effect. Carbohydrate rich foods with sufficient protein include whole grains, peas, lentils, barley, oats, beans and quinoa.

Reduce animal protein in diet. Why? When you consume natural high-carbohydrate foods without the presence of animal protein or fats, they allow tryptophan to flood the brain.

Ensure diet has enough iron. Why? Because the enzymes involved in the production of tryptophan and tyrosine contain iron which within the enzyme helps to regulate its activity. Iron is found in spinach, lentils sesame seeds and chickpeas.

Ensure diet is rich in magnesium and zinc which affect the activities of serotonin and dopamine. Natural foods rich in magnesium and zinc include pumpkin seeds, soya beans, spinach and quinoa.

Reduce consumption of unnatural food colorings and preservatives in your diet. These unnatural products affect the brain and have been found to increase ADHD symptoms in some people. I would recommend removing all artificial colorings and flavorings from your diet, although I know that this may be difficult for some of us, so at least remove the preservative sodium benzoate and the artificial colourings sunset yellow, quinoline yellow, tartrazine and allura red.

Exercise! Studies have proven over and over again that being physically active on a daily basis has a very positive effect on children with ADHD. Not only does it improve symptoms, being physically active also improves mood and cognitive performance. Even very light physical activity triggers the brain to release dopamine and serotonin which reduce ADHD symptoms.

Cognitive-Behavioral therapy which focuses on changing how one feels and acts by changing default thought patterns and persisting beliefs about oneself and about life is strongly recommended.

Cognitive-Behavioral Therapy also helps control anger and helps to stay focused.

## Chapter 27: Diets For Children With Adhd

How To Plan An Easy Simple Diet Which Is Effective

Give us a chance to face it. No one needs to boycott nourishments with manufactured shading, additives, sweeteners and flavorings since it turns into an outlandish errand! This is however the premise of the Feingold count calories which has been a standout amongst the most well known eating methodologies for children with ADHD. While there is proof to demonstrate that specific children with ADHD can undoubtedly profit by such an eating regimen, it is for the most part a hit and miss undertaking. Just on the grounds that every child is distinctive. As though we didn't have the foggiest idea!

Along these lines, when arranging diets for children with ADHD, I remember a couple of basic standards. I realize that an excess of sugar will bring about a sugar spike and later a crash as glucose levels abruptly fall. I know likewise that I can undoubtedly keep that crash just by including protein at breakfast. That can be cheddar or eggs for instance and can be given close by some basic starches so that there is sufficient to keep the child going for many hours.

My second straightforward standard is to ensure that there are sufficient Vitamin B components in my child's eating routine. Why? Since I realize that some Vitamin Bs like niacin which is Vitamin B3 truly help the cerebrum to capacity better. There are heaps of studies to demonstrate this and it is no mishap that scientists are utilizing this as a major aspect of the scan to discover a cure for Alzheimers illness.

What do I do? I ensure that there are loads of verdant green vegetables, meat, nuts, peanuts incorporated into the eating routine so that there is great mind fuel for the crucial cerebrum transmitters. It will help with ADHD symptoms and after some time, the child will have the capacity to focus better and have a greater attention traverse as well. On the off chance that we are truly fortunate, there will be less hyperactivity and fretfulness and for the most part there will be less troublesome conduct.

My last straightforward stride is to ensure that my child has enough Omega 3 fundamental unsaturated fats since I realize that 60% of the cerebrum is made of fat. I disregard all the favor angle since I realize that children don't by and large like that sustenance and furthermore that there are worries about mercury levels. I essentially locate a decent pharmaceutical review Omega 3 supplement to carry out the employment rather and it spares me a huge amount of cash and bother.

Along these lines, there you have it. We ought not overlook that weight control plans for children with ADHD are only one a player in an extensive program of treatment which incorporates conduct treatment, green time exercises, an organized and systematic family and possibly some pharmaceutical to help with hyperactivity.

As respects medicine, I have found that the best and most secure is homeopathy for ADHD which truly reestablishes quiet, great moods and peacefulness. On the off chance that that is truly what you need for your child, why not navigate and find how you can have more joyful family life again without worrying a lot about ADHD prescribed weight control plans.

Why not give YOUR child a superior shot in life? Find the certainties about a more normal and more secure approach which utilizes ADHD prescribed weight control plans and which can give you back your quietness and peace in the family home. Specialists now disclose to us that child conduct change consolidated with a characteristic treatment for ADHD is by a long shot the best ADHD treatment.

Time for Straight Talking

Diets for children with ADHD could be enormous business and possibly it will be soon. Possibly it will go an indistinguishable path from the pharmaceutical business which has "created" the ADHD disorder and promoted it so well that the figures have developed from 500,000 cases in 1985 to around 7 million children to-day. Leaving aside the vexed question of these psychostimulants, we need to inquire as to whether there are any ADHD suggested diets. Are eating methodologies for children with ADHD truly valuable or simply one more sidekick for the medication and nourishment industry ?

ADHD treatment runs as an inseparable unit with legitimate parental care at home and school. That implies investing energy with them and lessening media presentation (TV, PC Internet and recordings). At the point when guardians are truant this is called 'television child rearing' and it is a calming thought.

I don't put stock in ADHD prescribed eating regimens all things considered, however I do realize that specific nourishments can bring about unfavorably susceptible responses or may buildup them up with the goal that they begin skipping off the dividers. There is presently adequate proof from the EU and UK to bolster the restriction on certain sustenance colors which are known to intensify hyperactivity. The same goes for an excessive amount of sugar, salt, fat, caffeine and chocolate.

# Conclusion

Parenting is not the easiest job in the world, it is one of those things that you simply learn as you go along, but parenting a child with ADHD is even harder. Children with ADHD present numerous challenges for parents because their brains are wired differently than other children, they tend to act or speak without thinking. These children have no self-control, they are like a whirlwind of activity, and it seems nothing can stop them.

Parenting a child with ADHD can be difficult, but it is not impossible. Like other children, no one parenting technique is going to work with all children. You are going to have to try out different methods as you go through life. The one thing that you can count on though is the fact you must set clear rules for your children to follow and you must be consistent in enforcing those rules. Children with ADHD crave structure and routine, any deviation from their routines can cause total chaos to erupt in your household.

The point of this book was to help you see that when it comes to parenting children with ADHD there is no right or wrong way. Many parents have quite successfully adapted successfully parenting techniques. What you need to remember is that every child is different, so they will respond better to some techniques than others. The important thing is that you believe in yourself and your child.